The Quest for Wisdom

Essays in Honour of Philip Budd

Edited by

Christine E. Joynes

First published in 2002 by Orchard Academic, 16 Orchard Street, Cambridge, England, CB1 1JT

ISBN 190328305-1 (paper)

Cover: I.F. Rigaud. "Wisdom." London: J.&J. Boydell, 1799.

To Philip.

Contents

Preface   vii

Notes on Contributors   xi

1. Philip John Budd: An Appreciation   1
    Paul Joyce

2. Treasure in Heaven? Christina Rossetti's Use of   7
    Ecclesiastes
    Christine E. Joynes

3. Codifiability, Moral Wisdom, and the Foot/Hursthouse   29
    Thesis
    Stephen J. Boulter

4. 'The Holy of Holies': Something Queer in Reformist   53
    Political Theology
    Graeme Smith

5. The Mother of All The Buddhas   71
    Peggy Morgan

6. Body, Mind and Spirit: Westminster College's   89
    Contribution to Higher Education
    Tim Macquiban

7. The Wisdom of Clouds: Religious Responses to   109
   Environmental Issues in the Blue Mountains of
   New South Wales
   Richard Griffiths

8. Divine Wisdom: A Discourse of Christian Feminist   127
   Theology
   Angie Pears

9. Taking the Emperor's Clothes Seriously: The New   143
   Testament and the Roman Emperor
   Justin Meggitt

Preface

The essays in this volume are written in honour of Philip Budd, our esteemed colleague and friend. This book is offered as a token of appreciation for the friendship and support he has given us at various stages in the course of his teaching career, and it is also to mark and celebrate the occasion of his well-deserved retirement.

Philip has given unstinting loyalty to the institutions in which he has worked, retiring from Westminster College (which latterly became the Westminster Institute of Education) after over twenty years of service. In this context he has always enthusiastically joined in discussions with colleagues from all areas of theology, philosophy and religious studies. It is a testimony to Philip's friendship that representatives from all these areas have contributed to this book.

Philip's own area of expertise is biblical studies, but he has often adopted an interdisciplinary focus in his work; this is reflected, for example, in his most recent research on Qoheleth [Ecclesiastes] and Thomas Hardy. An interdisciplinary focus is also reflected in the essays in our volume. We have chosen wisdom as a uniting theme, primarily because it is a topic close to Philip's heart; but in addition, as several contributors note, wisdom is also a characteristic that many associate with Philip. From the discussion of political wisdom to an analysis of wisdom in Buddhism, it will become apparent that there are many interesting connections between the subjects that are covered.

In the opening chapter, Paul Joyce gives an appreciation of Philip's own work, highlighting not only his own contributions to scholarship but also his commitment to discussing the relevance of the Bible in the contemporary world. My own chapter, on Christina Rossetti's use of Ecclesiastes, explores some of the insights into biblical interpretation that can be derived from analysing the use of the Bible in literature. I suggest that a detailed investigation of Rossetti's use of Eccl. 1.2 'vanity of vanities! all is vanity' reveals significant correspondences between the book of

Ecclesiastes and the New Testament. This topic seemed a particularly appropriate one to explore here given Philip's own interest in relating the Bible to literature.

Stephen Boulter's chapter explores whether moral excellence and moral wisdom require a degree of intellectual sophistication not attainable by all. He argues that just as in science we rely on the authority of experts, so too in the moral realm this should be the case. There are interesting resonances between Boulter's contribution and the following chapter by Graeme Smith where again the role of 'experts' is addressed. Smith examines the nature of political wisdom and concludes that 'political theology might be either political or theological, but it should beware of seeking to be both together and ending up as neither'.

Peggy Morgan examines the role of wisdom in Buddhism in her chapter 'The Mother of All The Buddhas'. She highlights the rich interconnectedness between wisdom and other Buddhist concepts, such as compassion. The importance of this interdependence lies not least in its challenge to the stereotype of Buddhism as a path of wisdom in contrast to Christianity as a path of love.

In his chapter, Tim Macquiban explores the contribution Westminster College has made to higher education over the past one hundred and fifty years. He outlines the underlying aims of the institution and charts its shift from being a London-based Methodist College to its eventual merger with Oxford Brookes University in 2000. His analysis of the role of religion in secular education is particularly timely in view of the current debate about the subject.

Richard Griffiths draws our attention to the relationship between communities of religious practitioners and the ecosystems in which they exist in his contribution 'The Wisdom of Clouds'. He argues that 'religious discourse must develop an awareness of the ecological conditions of its own survival'. But, more radically, he asserts that religious truth claims should be tested against their ecological impact: 'The measure of religious truth is, at least, its impact on the natural environment in which that truth seeks to exist.'

In her contribution 'Divine Wisdom: A Discourse of Christian Feminist Theology' Angie Pears argues that it is time to move away from the question that has previously dominated theological debate, namely the compatibility of feminism and Christianity. Instead, she suggests attention needs to be directed to detailed 'evaluative study of the methodological mechanisms by which Christian theologies are informed by feminist values and critique'. She highlights the importance of the figure of Wisdom for feminists in their attempt to identify and recover potentially liberative aspects of the Christian tradition.

In the final contribution, 'Taking the Emperor's Clothes Seriously' Justin Meggitt re-evaluates the role of the Roman Emperor in the analysis of the New Testament. He demonstrates the significance of this neglected figure in the reception of early Christian texts and suggests a range of implications for our knowledge of the earliest churches.

Many people have helped in the process of seeing this book through to completion. In particular I would like to thank Janet Budd, Graham Cairns, Paul Joyce, Elaine Joynes, Nancy Macky, Justin Meggitt, Debbie Pinfold and Christopher Rowland for their invaluable assistance.

Christine E. Joynes
May 2002

Notes on Contributors

Stephen J. Boulter is Senior Lecturer in Philosophy and Ethics at the Westminster Institute of Education, Oxford Brookes University. He has a B.A.(Hons) and M.A. from the University of McMaster (Canada) and a Ph.D. from the University of Glasgow where he became Gifford Research Fellow in the Department of Philosophy. His research areas include the philosophy of language, the philosophy of science, theories of perception, metaphysics of value, Aristotle and medieval philosophy. Recent publications include 'Whose Challenge? Which Semantics?', *Synthese*, 126 (2001), pp. 325–37.

Richard Griffiths was Senior Chaplain at the Westminster Institute of Education (formerly Westminster College) until 2001. While there he established courses in environmental ethics and environmental theology. He is currently writing and raising his two young children in the Blue Mountains, Australia. Recent publications include 'Plotting Eden: Community Gardening in the 21st Century', in *Suburbia* (Sydney: National Trust of Australia (NSW), 2002).

Paul Joyce is Lecturer in Theology in the University of Oxford and a Fellow of St Peter's College. His work is on the Exilic Age of Ancient Israel (especially Ezekiel and Lamentations) and also on questions of method and biblical interpretation in the modern world. He and his wife, Alison, have two young daughters, both fans of Harry Potter. He was a colleague of Philip Budd at Ripon College Cuddesdon from 1980 to 1988.

Christine E. Joynes is Bampton Fellow in Theology at Trinity College, Oxford. She was formerly Lecturer in Biblical and Hermeneutical Studies at Westminster College, Oxford (1998 to 2001). Her research interests lie in the area of biblical interpretation, particularly the history of interpretation of Mark's gospel and the relationship between the Bible and culture. She is currently writing a commentary on Mark for the Blackwell series.

Tim Macquiban is Director of the Wesley and Methodist Studies Centre at the Westminster Institute of Education where he co-ordinates activities which continue the mission of the former Westminster College, teaches and supervises in areas of Church History and Liturgy and Ministerial Practice. His doctoral research was on Methodist attitudes to poverty in early nineteenth-century Britain.

Justin Meggitt is currently College Lecturer in Theology and Religious Studies at Corpus Christi College, Cambridge and Honorary Fellow of the Centre for Jewish–Christian Relations, Cambridge. He taught Biblical and Hermeneutical Studies with Philip at Westminster College, Oxford from 1994–1996. His primary research interest is in the relationship between ancient popular culture and earliest Christianity. He is the author of *Paul, Poverty and Survival* (1998) and *Christ and the Universe of Disease* (forthcoming).

Peggy Morgan was for many years a colleague of Philip Budd at Westminster College, where she lectured in the study of religions from 1977–2000. She is currently Lecturer in World Religions at Mansfield College, Oxford, a fellow of the Oxford Centre for Vaishnava and Hindu Studies, and Honorary President of the British Association for the Study of Religions. From 1996–2002 she was also Director of The Religious Experience Research Centre. Her recent published work includes *Six Religions in the Twenty-First Century* (edited with W Owen Cole, Stanley Thornes, 2000).

Angie Pears is Senior Lecturer in Practical and Contextual Theology at the Westminster Institute of Education, Oxford Brookes University. Her research interests are in the field of feminist theological discourse. Her recent publications focus on the methodological identity of Christian feminist theologies and she is currently writing a book on the strategies of feminist Christian encounter.

Graeme Smith is co-editor of the journal *Political Theology*. He was formerly Senior Lecturer in Social and Cultural Theology at the Westminster Institute of Education, Oxford Brookes University. He has edited books on mission and written on ecumenical and political theology. He is currently working on a project examining theology, political theory and history of religions.

Philip John Budd: An Appreciation

Paul Joyce

Philip Budd was born, like John Lennon and Cliff Richard, in 1940. His birth was on the night that the great medieval cathedral of Coventry was bombed. As the family home was near to the city centre, it was as well that his mother had been persuaded to move temporarily to her sister's in Loughborough. No sooner had Philip been baptized in Christ Church, Coventry, than that church too was devastated, forcing the congregation to move eventually to the parish of Cheylesmore where, as a teenager, Philip met one Janet Griffin, who would later become his wife.

After he finished school, Philip went to St John's College, Durham, to study Theology, and then, after a year spent teaching back in the Midlands in Rugby, he returned to Durham to train for the Anglican ministry at Cranmer Hall. It was at the start of this period, in 1963, that Philip married Janet, to whose constant support he owes so much. Among the many things they share are their radical political commitments and also music, especially jazz, which has led them regularly to the Upton-on-Severn Jazz Festival and numerous other musical events. Many speak of the contrast and complementarity of their styles and personalities as key factors in the success of their marriage. They celebrate their fortieth wedding anniversary in 2003.

Philip served as Curate in the Nottingham suburb of Chilwell from 1966 to 1969, after which he moved into theological education. Whilst maintaining a rich pastoral ministry, the teaching of the Old Testament was to be the major focus of his professional life. He taught at Clifton Theological College and then at its successor Trinity College, Bristol for eleven years in all, until 1980. During this time he completed in turn the M.Litt. of Durham University and the Ph.D. of Bristol University, the latter on the theme of the murmuring motif in the wilderness wandering narratives.

In 1980 Philip and Janet moved to Oxford, which has become their adopted home. From 1980 to 1988 Philip combined three jobs, as Tutor and Assistant Chaplain at Westminster College, Oxford, as Tutor at Ripon College Cuddesdon, and as Co-Director of the Oxford Institute for Church and Society, racing between these different responsibilities on his motorbike. It was typical of Philip to experiment with work patterns in this way, contributing richly in each corner of the triangle and making things work in an unfussy way. He bore the occasional marginalizing effects of such arrangements with good grace and typical strength of character. It was at Ripon College Cuddesdon that I got to know Philip, as fellow teacher of the Old Testament. He was a splendidly collaborative partner; he would do whatever was needed and his teaching was enormously appreciated, as was his preaching within the College community, recalled by one colleague as 'always original, insightful, memorable and challenging'. His work for the Oxford Institute for Church and Society, alongside Alastair Redfern, reflected another facet of his character, his passionate commitment to questions of social justice, evidenced also in his membership of the Labour Party at that time.

It was the third part of this pattern, Philip's work at Westminster College, Oxford, that was to develop into his full-time role as Lecturer there from 1988 until his retirement in 2001. Within the Church of England Philip had long moved easily between different traditions: in Bristol he had taught at an Evangelical theological college whilst worshipping at the Anglo-Catholic All Saints', Clifton. In his commitment over twenty years and more to the life and work of Westminster, a Methodist foundation, one saw the full extent of Philip's ecumenism. He regularly preached in the College Chapel and had an important pastoral as well as academic role in the College. This was combined with assisting in his local parish of North Hinksey.

Philip saw the College move from being a Methodist institution to being an integral part of the burgeoning Oxford Brookes University. Philip was in this context called upon to show his versatility and flexibility right up to the year of his retirement. He was keen to be part of new ventures within Brookes to promote the use of information technology in teaching and he actively contributed to an electronic discussion group that emerged out of a course on 'The Bible and Social Context'. He was particularly concerned to be totally *au fait* with the latest computer technology and even said that one of his ambitions was to become a computer 'whizz kid', though he added that maybe he had left it a bit late. Philip's wisdom and good humour sustained many during the far from easy Westminster/ Brookes merger. So for example, in the course of conversation about the merger, when colleagues were trying to grasp the intricacies of the modular system, Philip used as an illustration the study of 'Soft Furnishings and Theology' as a joint degree.

As an Old Testament scholar, Philip is a specialist on the Pentateuch and more especially its Priestly elements. Alongside his many duties Philip has seen through to completion two substantial commentaries, which combine depth of scholarship with breadth of perspective. The completion of these two major volumes signals long-term disciplined dedication to scholarship in the midst of a life that has yielded all too few opportunities for extended research and writing time. In 1984 the Word Bible Commentary on *Numbers* appeared,[1] and in 1996 the New Century Bible volume on *Leviticus*, some words from which well summarize the subtlety and the humanity of Philip's biblical scholarship: 'It is precisely because of its ambiguities and the ways in which they accurately reflect the enigmatic character of human motivation and experience, that Leviticus deserves to be taken seriously theologically. A theology which fails to grasp such "nettles" will ultimately fail in its endeavour.'[2] He has often contributed also at a more popular level, as for example in his entries for *The Lion Handbook to the Bible*.[3]

Philip brings to his Old Testament work a rich breadth of methods, eclectic but disciplined and reflective. He has commented that he believes the historical-critical approach is indispensable for biblical study, but he is also more than open to exploring new approaches. His important article on 'Holiness and Cult' in *The World of Ancient Israel* reflects a characteristic openness to the insights of the human sciences, an interest that has grown steadily over the years.[4] Bill Bellinger has compared and contrasted Philip's two biblical commentaries. The way he does so in part reflects his own agenda, but it also accurately highlights Philip's developing indebtedness to the insights of the social sciences. Of the later Leviticus commentary, Bellinger writes that it 'concentrates on cultural codes that can help readers glimpse how ancient auditors could have heard or read this text and which can help contemporary readers comprehend the unfamiliar world this Priestly text is commending'.[5] Philip is indeed very interested in discussing the relevance of the Bible in our contemporary context, and in hermeneutical issues, such as the question of the authority of the Bible. The emphasis in many of his biblical studies courses on the interpretation of the Bible in the modern world reflects Philip's concern to relate his academic work to wider society. Such concerns are particularly to the fore in the new commentary on Numbers that Philip has produced, almost twenty years on from his first.[6]

Philip is no narrow biblical scholar. His love of literature, especially Thomas Hardy, informs so much that he does. And this is a scholarly as well as a personal interest, as is indicated by his attendance since the nineteen seventies at various Hardy conferences, notably the biennial Summer School at Dorchester, Hardy's birthplace. Philip also interrelates the various parts of his intellectual life. He recently read a paper on 'Qoheleth (Ecclesiastes) and Thomas Hardy' at the Oxford Old Testament Seminar, and at Westminster he taught a course on 'Biblical Interpretation and Thomas Hardy' that was particularly popular with students. In a period when 'literary approaches' to reading the Bible have become fashionable, few engage in this with the genuine familiarity with and love of literature that Philip does. He communicates his passion for Hardy to others very effectively. It was Philip who eventually got me to read *Jude the Obscure*. The pathos and depth of human sympathy of that great work are close to the heart of Philip. He is a man familiar with vulnerability, one thinks of his long-term hearing difficulty, or again of the recent death of his younger brother John, the victim of a brain tumour. Such experiences are transformed by Philip into a sensitive care of those around him. 'A lovely man' is the way more than one person has described him. Friends and colleagues alike know him as a gentle, eirenical, unassuming and modest person, who is at the same time strong and stable, a great enabler and supporter of others. We know him perhaps above all as a wise man, much loved and highly respected, and it is in this spirit that we offer the present collection of essays gathered around the theme of wisdom.

When asked recently what he planned to do when he retired, Philip replied that in an ideal world he would work in the Oxfam bookshop in the mornings and in the Bodleian Library in the afternoons, an answer that reflects beautifully his twin commitments to social justice and to learning. But however he spends his time, we wish Philip a long and very happy retirement.

Notes

1. P. J. Budd, *Numbers*, Word Biblical Commentary (Waco, TX: Word, 1984).
2. P. J. Budd, *Leviticus*, New Century Bible Commentary (London: Marshall Pickering / Grand Rapids, MI: Eerdmans, 1996), p. viii.
3. P. J. Budd, 'The Sacrificial System' and 'Feasts and Festivals', in D. and P. Alexander (eds.), *The Lion Handbook to the Bible* (Tring: Lion Publishing, 1973), pp. 174–5 and pp. 180–1.
4. P. J. Budd, 'Holiness and Cult', in R. E. Clements (ed.), *The World of Ancient Israel: Sociological, Anthropological and Political Perspectives, Essays by Members of the Society for Old Testament Study* (Cambridge: Cambridge University Press, 1989), pp. 275–98.
5. W. H. Bellinger, Jr., 'Enabling Silent Lips to Speak: Literary Criticism in the Service of Old Testament Interpretation', in E. Ball (ed.), *In Search of True Wisdom: Essays in Old Testament Interpretation in Honour of Ronald E. Clements*, JSOT Supplement Series 300 (Sheffield: Sheffield Academic Press, 1999), p. 63.
6. P. J. Budd, 'Numbers', in J. D. G. Dunn and J. W. Rogerson (eds.), *Eerdmans Bible Commentary* (Grand Rapids, MI: Eerdmans, forthcoming).

Treasure in Heaven? Christina Rossetti's Use of Ecclesiastes

Christine E. Joynes

> Do not lay up for yourselves treasures on earth, where moth and rust consume and where thieves break in and steal, but lay up for yourselves treasure in heaven, where neither moth nor rust consumes and where thieves do not break in and steal. For where your treasure is, there will be your heart also. (Matthew 6.19–21)

Introduction

Analysis of how the Bible has been used in literature is a much-neglected field of study, yet it is one that yields rich treasures, offering new insights into biblical interpretation.[1] The Bible is a dynamic text which has been interpreted in a multitude of ways over the centuries; it is not static and unchanging, simply yielding a single meaning which transcends all times and cultures. Poets and novelists are therefore part of a stream of people who have applied the Bible to their own contexts.

In this chapter I will explore Christina Rossetti's use of the book of Ecclesiastes, focusing specifically upon her use of Eccl. 1.2 'vanity of vanities! all is vanity' and examining the contribution she makes to its interpretation. This in turn will raise broader questions about the nature of the biblical text and contexts of interpretation. Rossetti's work indicates that there are both significant continuities and differences in the interpretation of Ecclesiastes during its reception history. By exploring her poetry, the dynamic nature of biblical interpretation – where the text itself becomes transfigured – will be illustrated.

Part 1: Christina Rossetti in Context

All biblical interpreters are influenced by their contexts; Rossetti is no exception and we therefore begin by examining her biographical and historical contexts. Christina Rossetti (1830–94) was born in London, the youngest of four children, with an Italian father and an Italian-English mother. Her family was artistic and literary: her sister published on Dante, and her two brothers were leading figures in the Pre-Raphaelite brotherhood. Christina displayed similar talent, publishing work in a range of different genres: sonnets, love lyrics, children's rhymes, short stories and devotional readings are amongst some of the forms she used. By all accounts her family context was happy, with deep affection among siblings and parents evident.

Two particular themes from Christina Rossetti's biographical context have been highlighted by commentators because of alleged influence on her poetry. The first is the theme of unfulfilled love. In 1850 Rossetti broke off her engagement to the Pre-Raphaelite painter James Collinson because he reverted to his former Catholic faith. Subsequently, in 1866, she refused the marriage proposal of Charles Cayley, probably on account of his religious scepticism.[2] Throughout her life Rossetti remained single. This biographical knowledge has led many critics to argue that her poetry reflects a sense of frustration at unfulfilled love and fears about spinsterhood.[3] However, this biographical eisegesis has been overemphasized and ignores the contrasting moods in Rossetti's poetry.

The second key theme is the ill-health Rossetti suffered and which some scholars believe lies behind her preoccupation with death. According to her brother William's memoir, she suffered severe health problems during her youth, though the causes are not clear.[4] In addition, during her early forties she developed Graves' disease, a disfiguring illness. These health problems may have contributed to what is often referred to as a morbid or melancholy strain in her poetry. We would be mistaken, though, if we caricatured Rossetti's poetry as merely a reflection of her personal views on love and death. As the discussion below reveals, the rich variety in her work prevents us from interpreting her poetry as a straightforward representation of the poet's own *persona*.

Rossetti is frequently described as a quiet recluse, but this overlooks the many and varied activities in which she was involved during her life.[5] She had contact with contemporary poets and artists, so should with its not be regarded as someone who was totally detached from worldly affairs. On two occasions she assisted her mother in setting up a school, though neither venture was successful. Her social conscience found an outlet through her work at a home for 'fallen women', and she also campaigned against cruelty to animals. These activities militate against portrayals of Rossetti as a figure who shunned involvement in the world.

Beyond the immediate biographical context, we must also consider Rossetti's wider historical context. Faith and doubt are two terms often used to define the Victorian period in which Rossetti lived. It was an age of 'progress', where long-held traditional religious values were being challenged both by scientific discovery, epitomized in Darwin's *Origin of Species* (1859) and by intellectual developments, such as the advent of 'Higher Criticism' of the biblical text. The Victorian period was therefore one of change, upheaval and diversity. This diversity was apparent in the spectrum of religious persuasions in Rossetti's own household: her father a free-thinking Catholic, her brothers both atheists and her mother and sister both High Church Anglicans, like herself.

In contrast to the prevailing mood of Victorian scepticism, Rossetti tends to be portrayed as a saintly, pious figure.[6] It is, however, highly questionable whether this accurately reflects Rossetti's personal beliefs.[7] Victorian scepticism may perhaps be one context which explains her choice of Ecclesiastes as a favourite text.[8] According to J. J. McGann, 'The style of her verse is simple, chaste, and severe, but it is also recognizably in a Victorian stylistic tradition, and in that respect it is "orthodox".'[9] But the extent of her orthodoxy is perhaps a more open question when we acknowledge the prominence of Ecclesiastes in her work and how she uses it.

A further influence from the religious climate is the Oxford Movement, with its doctrine of reserve. As G. B. Tennyson comments:

> The idea of reserve is that since God is ultimately incomprehensible, we can know Him only indirectly; His truth is hidden and given to us only in a manner suited to our capacities for apprehending it. Moreover, it is both unnecessary and undesirable that God and religious truth generally should be disclosed in their fullness at once to all regardless of the differing capacities of individuals to apprehend such things.[10]

This reserve provides another reason for Rossetti's attraction to

Ecclesiastes, with its clear sense of life's complexity and challenge to earthly endeavours, though we should note that the book is not prominent amongst other Tractarian poets such as Keble, Newman or Isaac Williams.

McGann has drawn attention to the premillenarian context in which Rossetti lived, suggesting that this also had a significant impact upon her.[11] In particular he appeals to the influence of the premillenarian doctrine of soul sleep, a waiting time between death and the second coming. He identifies this as a theme throughout Rossetti's poetry and goes so far as to say:

> This premillenarian concept is the single most important enabling principle in Rossetti's religious poetry. By this I mean that no other idea generated such a network of poetic possibilities for her verse, that no other idea contributed so much to the concrete and specific character of her work.[12]

But, the centrality of this theme in her poetry is debatable; for example, in the selection of poems we consider below it is totally absent. Therefore, in contrast to McGann's argument that this doctrine underlies Rossetti's emphasis on the theme of vanity of vanities, we illustrate that in her use of Eccl. 1.2 the doctrine of soul sleep does not come to the fore.

McGann observes that Rossetti's poetry provides 'an oblique glimpse into the heaven and the hell of late Victorian England as that world was mediated through the particular experiences of Christina Rossetti'.[13] This highlights the significance of both the wider historical context and the poet's own particular circumstances upon her work. We will see from examining her use of Ecclesiastes that far from the suggestion Victorian poetry served 'as merely a tool for religious propaganda, sugaring the pill of dry dogma and doctrinal proposition', rather her despair about earthly existence *contrasts* with traditional orthodox piety, whilst nevertheless having a biblical basis.[14]

The prominence of the Bible in Christina Rossetti's work is widely acknowledged.[15] Indeed, the useful concordance compiled by Jiménez records the relative frequency with which Rossetti uses particular biblical passages.[16] This high dependence on the Bible is generally attributed to her piety, reflecting her High Church background. Yet Rossetti's use of the Bible, though acknowledged, is seldom explored in detail. If her use of Eccl. 1.2 is mentioned, the assumption is that this reflects the general melancholy tenor the poet adopts in her writing. In the following section we will see, however, that Rossetti interprets Ecclesiastes in a range of ways. She does not simply adopt a single, straightforward stance, nor is her use of Ecclesiastes uniformly melancholy.

Our survey of Christina Rossetti in context has highlighted a significant question: *to what extent should we use biographical knowledge about Rossetti to interpret her poetry?* It is a question which has been hotly debated. McGann rightly argues that the biographical context of Rossetti's work has been overly exaggerated.[17] Whilst some contextual information is useful, we must also let the poems speak for themselves.

Part 2: Christina Rossetti and Ecclesiastes

Before launching into an analysis of Rossetti's use of Ecclesiastes, we need to briefly outline the contemporary critical thinking about Ecclesiastes which was prominent during her lifetime, to provide a means of contrast. Of particular interest is Ginsburg's commentary, *Coheleth, Commonly Called the Book of Ecclesiastes* (1861).

Two critical issues are noteworthy. First, the canonicity of Ecclesiastes was frequently commented upon, with commentators puzzling over how such a pessimistic text ever made it into the Christian canon. In addition, the date and provenance of the text were contested.[18] Secondly, the tensions and inconsistencies in the book were perceived to be problematic, leading some commentators to attribute parts of Ecclesiastes to a later glossator. According to Ginsburg, 'Few books in the Bible have given rise to greater diversities of opinion than Coheleth.'[19] Seeking to reconcile the various tensions, scholars proposed summaries of the message of Ecclesiastes; many highlighted the encouragement in the book to live life to the full as it was a gift of God. 'There is nothing left for man but the enjoyment of things of this world in his possession, being the gift of God to the righteous.'[20] This can be contrasted with Rossetti's approach which we will now consider.

To my knowledge, no detailed investigation of Rossetti's use of Ecclesiastes has been undertaken in spite of the prominence of this text in her work; it is one of the biblical books which Rossetti quotes most often. Although fruitful discussion could emerge from exploring Rossetti's use of the whole of Ecclesiastes, for our present purposes we will confine our attention to the use she makes of Eccl. 1.2 ('vanity of vanities! all is vanity'), a theme which often leads her to illustrate with further Ecclesiastes passages.[21]

'Vanity of vanities! all is vanity' is her favourite phrase from the book.[22] Rossetti is not the first to apply this cry of despair to literature but her extensive use of the text is striking.[23] She explicitly quotes it in fourteen of her poems and she even names two poems after this verse.[24] McGann recognizes the prominence of this text in her work: 'Christina Rossetti's notorious obsession with the theme of the world's vanity lies at the root of her refusal to compromise with her age or to adopt reformist positions … [Her] *contemptus mundi* is the basis of her critical freedom and poetic illumination.'[25] Therefore Ecclesiastes provides the poet with a means of criticizing her world.

Sometimes the sentiments of Eccl. 1.2 appear even where the verse is not explicitly quoted. The challenge to distinguish between the real and the illusory is a key theme throughout her work. For example, many of Rossetti's characters are placed in situations where they are asked to make this distinction between reality and illusion, as in the poem 'May'.[26] The theme of *vanitas vanitatum* transcends the division between 'devotional' and 'non-devotional' poems, it permeates her entire corpus. As mentioned above, vanity is used by Rossetti in different ways. To illustrate this we will now compare a selection of her poems.

Rossetti's poem 'A Testimony' (1849) is one of the most significant poems in which she focuses on Ecclesiastes. It begins with a clear statement of contempt for the world:

> I said of laughter: it is vain.
> Of mirth I said: what profits it?
> Therefore I found a book, and writ
> Therein how ease and also pain,
> How health and sickness, every one
> Is vanity beneath the sun[27]

The speaker is Solomon, the king of Jerusalem mentioned in the final stanza, who is described as 'the wisest man on earth'.[28] In spite of his wisdom and all the wealth at his disposal, this great figure still reaches the conclusion that:

> All things are vanity, I said:
> Yea, vanity of vanities.

The frequent occurrence of the term 'vanity', found six times in this poem together with three additional uses of the adjective 'vain', is striking. In the first two stanzas these terms occur four times within the space of eight lines. Vanity is stressed from the outset and dominates the whole poem. Of particular note is the repetitive emphasis that *all* is vanity.

When the theme of vanity is introduced in the opening stanza it is defined by a collection of various passages from Ecclesiastes.[29] But, significantly, vanity is then linked to the Matthean parable about storing treasure in heaven rather than on earth (Mtt. 6.19–21) in the third stanza:

> Our treasures moth and rust corrupt,
> Or thieves break thro' and steal, or they
> Make themselves wings and fly away.

Rossetti here connects passages in the Old and New Testaments; but she also elaborates further, associating the underlying sentiment from Ecclesiastes with other gospel parables, namely the parable of the man who stores up treasure for himself in barns (Lk. 12.16–21) and the parable of the man who built his house upon the sand (Mtt. 7.24–27):

> One man made merry as he supped,
> Nor guessed how when that night grew dim
> His soul would be required of him.
>
> We build our houses on the sand
> Comely withoutside and within;
> But when the winds and rains begin
> To beat on them they cannot stand:
> They perish, quickly overthrown,
> Loose from the very basement stone.

This rich intertextual interplay is characteristic of Rossetti's work. Her appeal to these three gospel parables clearly indicates that for her the key is to store up treasure in heaven and not on earth. By making this connection between the wisdom tradition of Ecclesiastes and the parables of Jesus in the gospels, Rossetti here anticipates a twentieth-century development in New Testament scholarship, with its emphasis on Jesus as a cynic.[30]

'Treasure in heaven' can be interpreted both positively and negatively. On the one hand, anticipation of 'treasure in heaven' provides hope of a future inheritance; on the other, the treasure is in heaven and not on earth, which therefore leads to a negative understanding of earthly existence in her poetry. Indeed, in many poems the future hope is totally eclipsed and the focus is purely on rejection of worldly pleasure (see for example the discussion of 'One Certainty' below).

In the fifth stanza Rossetti focuses upon death's inevitability ('All in the end shall have but dust'). The mood shifts, however, in the sixth stanza, with its reference to the period after death, introducing the future tense for the first time in the poem:

> The one inheritance, which best
> And worst alike shall find and share:
> The wicked cease from troubling there,
> And there the weary be at rest;
> There all the wisdom of the wise
> Is vanity of vanities.

The reference here to a future inheritance introduces a more positive note, though the theme of vanity is still retained; it is now used to indicate that worldly wisdom will not count for anything in this future situation. There is something subversive about the emphasis here, rejecting worldly wisdom (a theme found in the gospels: see for example Mtt. 11.25). The inheritance is mentioned again, implicitly, in the tenth stanza again with the future tense:

> He who hath little shall not lack;
> He who hath plenty shall decay

Characteristically, Rossetti appeals to the natural world to illustrate the transience of life. She hereby rejects the Romantic notion of close communion with nature and instead focuses upon detachment from the natural world.[31]

'Vanity of vanities' is interpreted by Jiménez to mean, 'life is a weary monotony from which there seems to be no deliverance in this world'.[32] He suggests that this reflects Rossetti's own personal sense of despair. But as we have seen above, we also need to acknowledge the note of hope in her poetry, signified in this poem by the reference to a future

14

inheritance and implied by her use of three gospel parables whose emphasis is on treasure in heaven. We might also note at this point that her attraction to the theme of treasure in heaven and Ecclesiastes can be related to her repulsion from Victorian attitudes of spending and acquiring.[33] McGann suggests that the theme 'vanity of vanities' functions for Rossetti as a 'vehicle for understanding … certain institutionalized patterns of social destructiveness operating in nineteenth-century England'.[34]

Another poem in which the theme of Eccl. 1.2 is prominent is 'One Certainty' (1849). This can be contrasted with the poem 'A Testimony' since it lacks the positive allusion to treasure in heaven; instead the one certainty referred to in the title is the inevitability of death ('all things end in the long dust of death'). The poem opens with a reference to the pessimism of Eccl. 1.2:

> Vanity of vanities, the Preacher saith,
> All things are vanity.

Its position at the beginning of the poem underlines its importance for everything to follow. This quotation is conjoined with two further quotations from Ecclesiastes in the poem: firstly from Eccl. 1.8 ('The eye and ear / Cannot be filled with what they see and hear') and also Eccl. 1.9 ('And there is nothing new under the sun').

Again Rossetti appeals to nature for an example of the transience of life; she also displays her intertextual approach by using Isa. 40.7–8 when elaborating on this motif ('like the grass that withereth'). Whereas in Ecclesiastes 'the Preacher' encourages his audience to enjoy life, nothing of this message is retained in the poem. Quite the opposite: Rossetti emphasizes that people gain little joy from earthly existence. The only faint glimmer of hope that might be detected in the poem is in the phrase '*Until* the ancient race of Time be run' suggesting that at this point things will change. However, there is no reference made to heaven or a future inheritance, ideas evident in other Rossetti poems.

The contrast between 'A Testimony' and 'One Certainty' illustrates the variety of ways in which Rossetti responds to the text of Eccl. 1.2. A further example of this contrast can be found when we consider her poem 'Vanity of Vanities' (1847) which takes its title from Eccl. 1.2. This poem is spoken in the first person singular and the speaker is again Solomon, the figure (otherwise referred to as 'the Preacher') with whom she always associates the phrase 'vanity of vanities'. The poem opens with a cry of despair, for the speaker has discovered that pleasure is vain. The emphasis on this theme at the beginning and end of the poem indicates its significance. The reference to a 'glory that is past' may reflect apocryphal traditions about Solomon's demise.

Again this poem portrays the same bleak outlook that we found in the poem 'One Certainty', lacking the hopeful assurance we discovered in 'A Testimony'. Moreover, as in 'One Certainty' an element of change is to be found in the future focus in the poem, with its reference to 'at the last'. This is emphasized by the repetition of the phrase in two consecutive lines. A future transformation may also be implied in the line,

so again / It shall say *till* the mighty angel-blast.[35]

Nevertheless, even after this allusion, pessimism returns in the reference to men 'evermore' going fearfully. Rossetti's intertextual method is again employed, but she subverts the theme from Isaiah; instead of young men rising up from their weariness on eagle's wings (Isa 40.31) according to this poem, 'even the young shall answer sighingly, / Saying to one another: How vain it is!'; this refers to the vanity of pleasure.

The use of Eccl. 1.2 in the poem 'The Lowest Room' (1856) is different again from the texts we have so far considered. This poem is a dialogue between two sisters, focusing on the contrast between their two substantially different views about life. It is written from the perspective of the elder sister whose negative view contrasts starkly with the more positive outlook of her younger sister. The title of the poem comes from the emphasis on the elder sister taking the lowest place. Indeed it is in the context of meditating on this theme that the first reference to vanity occurs:

"Some must be second and not first;
All cannot be the first of all:
Is not this, too, but vanity?
I stumble like to fall."

Rivalry between the two sisters is apparent throughout the poem, with its contrast between both their physical features and their mental dispositions. The elder sister's bleak outlook is emphasized in the second stanza:

> "Oh what is life, that we should live?
> Or what is death, that we must die?
> A bursting bubble is our life:
> I also, what am I?"

It is further underlined by her subsequent references to 'aimless life' and 'blank life'. The younger sister picks up the latter reference and turns it around by responding:

> "Our life is given us as a blank;
> Ourselves must make it blest or curst"

In view of the description of the younger sister's mild temperament, it is somewhat surprising to find that she disagrees with her elder sister's views on several occasions.

The debate between the two women begins by considering whether former times were better than the present (a position held by the elder sister and refuted by the younger). An explicitly religious dimension is introduced part way through the poem by the younger sister who dismisses the example of Homer in favour of the model provided by Christ. In response to this religious position the elder sister is not to be beaten; at this point she also turns to religion and appeals to the example of Solomon, 'the wisest man of all the wise' who,

> Left for his summary of life
> 'Vanity of vanities'.

Perhaps the elder sister hopes that the biblical basis of this example will carry more weight with her younger sister (though she does admit that she makes the comment 'half bitter, half in jest'). In three successive stanzas she quotes from Ecclesiastes, emphasizing Solomon's dismissal of *all* as vanity of vanities and concluding:

> If I am wearied of my life,
> Why so was Solomon.

The third of these stanzas is heavy with repetition, as if by repeating the phrase 'vanity of vanities' the speaker is trying to convince us of the truth of her position. She tries to connect this biblical emphasis to her earlier argument, shifting from her former description of Homer and instead asserting that his victories reflected the transience of which Solomon spoke. The younger sister is not persuaded by the appeal to Solomon's pessimism and refutes the example from Ecclesiastes by her self-effacing comment: 'One is here … yea, / Greater than Solomon' (Mtt. 12.42). Again Rossetti uses an intertextual approach in her poem, but in this instance an Old Testament example (Solomon) is superseded by a New Testament figure ('one greater than Solomon').

Although this discussion does not occur exactly in the middle of the poem, it does mark an impasse in the argument, the point at which both sisters fall silent. The younger sister has triumphed. The theme of wisdom, raised by the reference to Solomon, is continued with the younger sister described as 'intuitively wise', something which the elder sister recognizes cannot be imparted by books.

This use of the Ecclesiastes text demonstrates Rossetti's versatility in applying the phrase 'vanity of vanities'. The mood of this poem is markedly different from the more pessimistic 'One Certainty' and 'Vanity of Vanities' in spite of the common thread of Eccl. 1.2 linking these texts. The concluding section of the poem marks some changes and some continuities: the elder sister does not alter her view of life ('year after tedious year') in spite of eventually resigning herself to not being first. However, in contrast to the earlier part of the poem, she now displays some of the religious devotion which was previously associated with her younger sister. For example, she cites Psalm 121 ('I lift my eyes up to the hills / From whence my hope shall come').

The key theme in this poem is about who is first or last. The concluding stanza perhaps undermines the elder sister's statement that she has eventually learned not to be first, since here she expresses her hope for a future reversal of fortunes:

> Yea, sometimes still I lift my heart
> To the Archangelic trumpet-burst,
> When all deep secrets shall be shown,
> And many last be first.

This reflects the anticipation of heavenly reversal expressed elsewhere by

Rossetti in her use of the Eccl. 1.2 theme.

The final poem in our selection is 'Saints and Angels' (1875). This has the most positive stance towards the future life beyond death that we have encountered thus far. The poem opens with a clear expression of the speaker's longing to escape bodily existence:

> It's oh in Paradise that I fain would be,
> Away from earth and weariness and all beside

The second and third stanzas then focus on the joy of heavenly existence. The theme of lovers who will be reunited in heaven is one which is introduced in the fourth stanza and recurs throughout the poem. Rossetti mentions the transience of life here but she contrasts this with the abiding nature of love:

> This life is but the passage of a day,
> This life is but a pang and all is over,
> But in the life to come which fades not away
> Every love shall abide and every lover.

We can compare this emphasis on the endurability of love with the poem 'In the Willow Shade' (1881) where the poet comments:

> All things are vain that wax and wane,
> For which we waste our breath;
> Love only doth not wane and is not vain,
> Love only outlives death.

This contrasts with the dismissal of *all* as vanity in other poems, where no exceptions are made.

In the poem 'Saints and Angels' we find continued emphasis on the futility of earthly pleasure and wisdom in the sixth and seventh stanzas, with further allusions to Ecclesiastes. Solomon is described as a figure who 'wore out pleasure and mastered all lore', recording that prior to death all was 'vanity of vanities':

> With loves by the hundred, wealth beyond measure,
> Is this he, who wrote "Vanity of vanities"?
> Yea, "Vanity of vanities" he saith of pleasure,

And of all he learned set his seal to this.

In contrast to the previous poems, such as 'One Certainty', where the poet has endorsed the conclusion of Ecclesiastes, here a different approach is taken, distinguishing between 'us' and Solomon:

> Yet we love and faint not, for our love is one,
> And we hope and flag not, for our hope is sure

The poet appeals to her audience not to be troubled by the inevitable approach of death; the conclusion reiterates the positive expectation that lovers will be reunited in heaven, 'And Paradise hath room for you and me and all'. This universalistic emphasis, with room in heaven for all, can be found elsewhere in Rossetti's poetry.[36]

This brief examination of a selection of Christina Rossetti's poems which explicitly quote Eccl. 1.2 has illustrated the diversity in her use of the biblical text. The most significant theme to emerge is the connection between the despair in Ecclesiastes and the New Testament hope of treasure in heaven. This emphasis challenges traditional labelling of Rossetti's work as 'melancholy', reflecting total despair; it ignores the element of hope in many of her poems. Moreover, the differing moods in Rossetti's poems cannot be explained simply in terms of chronological progression, since some of the contrasting poems we examined above were written in the same year. Our investigation also questions McGann's argument for the prominence of the doctrine of soul sleep in Rossetti's work; we did not find this theme in any of the poems we discussed. It is therefore highly doubtful that this is the basis for her emphasis on 'vanity of vanities'. A final point to note is the interpretative mileage Rossetti makes out of the fact that she regards Solomon as the author of Ecclesiastes. Whilst the connection between Solomon and Ecclesiastes is generally rejected and ignored by the scholarly community, the interpretative possibilities offered by this association have been significant in the reception history of Ecclesiastes.[37]

Part 3: Context and Interpretation

We acknowledged earlier some features from Rossetti's biographical and historical contexts which may have influenced her interpretation of Eccl. 1.2. However, whilst recognizing contextual relevance we should also note some features of Rossetti's interpretation of Ecclesiastes shared by other interpreters, indicating that they are therefore not necessarily tied only to her context.

The strong emphasis in Rossetti's poetry on renouncing the world and all its pleasures has been interpreted by some commentators as simply a reflection of her biographical context, indicating female resignation. This overlooks the wider context of Church tradition and prior interpretation of Ecclesiastes. For example, figures like Jerome in the patristic period clearly explored Ecclesiastes from an ascetical point of view, suggesting that the text challenges people to shun the world.

When we compare this ascetic interpretation with the text of Ecclesiastes itself some interesting points emerge. Alongside its emphasis on the vanity of human endeavours, Ecclesiastes also clearly promotes enjoyment of the pleasures of the world, a feature which is totally neglected in Rossetti's work.[38] One might argue that she is hereby being deliberately selective in her use of Ecclesiastes (a text which is notoriously contradictory). Rossetti, like other commentators before her, is perhaps here domesticating the text. Appealing to the history of interpretation of Ecclesiastes is not to deny that Rossetti did adopt an ascetic approach to life personally; but attention to the wider understanding of Ecclesiastes illustrates that an ascetic interpretation is not purely her personal subjective reading of the text.

Rossetti's asceticism also informs our interpretation of her views on death, another prominent theme in her poetry. The focus on death was a typically Victorian theme, but it may also be linked to her own ill-health.[39] The liberation provided by the afterlife is a key theme in her work.[40] As noted above, this is in stark contrast to the emphasis of Ecclesiastes on death's finality.

Another interesting feature surfaces when we compare Rossetti's poem 'A Testimony' with a poem by Anne Bradstreet 'The Vanity of All Worldly Things'. Bradstreet was writing much earlier than Rossetti; her poems were published in the mid-seventeenth century.[41] In her poem 'The Vanity of All Worldly Things', cited by Atwan and Wieder in their book *Chapters into Verse*, there are certain significant similarities with Rossetti's work.[42] Not least, both poets link the theme of 'vanity of vanities' with the idea of storing up treasure in heaven, not on earth:

What is't in wealth great treasures to obtain?
No, that's but labor, anxious care and pain.
He heaps up riches and he heaps up sorrow,
It's his today, but who's his heir tomorrow? [43]

Bradstreet also refers to the significance of Solomon as author of Ecclesiastes, commenting that this 'wisest man of men' simply found 'vanity, vexation of the mind'. A third feature shared by Bradstreet and Rossetti is the element of future hope in the face of this vanity. Bradstreet describes this in terms of a path leading to a crystal fount. She too includes an element of subversion, by commenting that those who follow this path are not given any recognition by the world.

This raises interesting questions: to what extent was there a common thread between these two poets (had Rossetti read Bradstreet?), or was this connection self-evident from a Christian perspective? These are the only two authors I have come across so far who have made this connection between Ecclesiastes and the New Testament theme of treasure in heaven, maybe there are others to be discovered. The parallels between Rossetti and Bradstreet further challenge McGann's interpretation of Rossetti's emphasis on *vanitas vanitatum*, since he correlates this with a specifically mid-nineteenth-century premillenarian context not shared by Bradstreet.[44]

Part 4: Conclusions

In this chapter I have indicated some possible connections between Rossetti's own personal and historical contexts and her interpretation of Eccl. 1.2. This is an apt reminder of the role context plays in one's interpretation of the Bible. On the other hand, we have also seen some important continuities in the interpretation of Ecclesiastes which indicate that biblical interpretation is not solely bound by one's context, but is part of an ongoing tradition. This was highlighted first by comparing Rossetti's ascetic understanding of Ecclesiastes with the ascetic interpretation of Jerome and secondly by highlighting the similarities between Rossetti and Bradstreet in their association of Ecclesiastes with a hope for treasure in heaven.

Rossetti's use of Ecclesiastes also provides us with one example of how readers have dealt with the perceived tensions within the book. It is noteworthy that whilst there is variation in the way Rossetti uses Eccl. 1.2, there is also a certain consistency in her interpretation of the book: she never adopts its alternative emphasis on enjoying this life because that is all there is.

A further contribution of Rossetti's work to biblical studies is through the rich intertextuality which she employs. By connecting Ecclesiastes with the hope for treasure in heaven, Rossetti thereby implicitly raises questions about the place of Ecclesiastes within the *Christian* canon. Her poetry forces us to ask: how else can we interpret Ecclesiastes in the Christian canon apart from by relating it to the New Testament hope for a future inheritance? Rossetti's use of biblical traditions is therefore somewhat subversive, transforming Ecclesiastes in the light of Christian hope for life beyond death.

The intertextuality we find in Rossetti's poetry should also alert us to the importance of relating the Old and New Testaments even where explicit citations are lacking. Too often biblical critics have overlooked connections between Ecclesiastes and the New Testament, since Ecclesiastes is only explicitly alluded to once in it (Rom. 8.20). As Fiddes points out, poetry awakens the reader to new correspondences: 'The poet asks, in effect, "Have you noticed that this is like that?" … By bringing two verbal signs together in an image, new levels of meaning are given to both.'[45]

In conclusion: 'Each generation has both re-written and been re-written, by the seemingly continuous dialectic between the Bible and its age.'[46] Christina Rossetti is one example of how this interactive process took place in the Victorian period. Exploring such processes is essential to assist the broader discussion in biblical studies about what the text might mean and how it can be interpreted.

Notes

1. This neglect has been addressed to some extent through the work of David Jasper and Stephen Prickett. See for example D. Jasper and S. Prickett, *The Bible and Literature. A Reader* (Oxford: Blackwell, 1999). However, there is still much scope for further research.

2. William Rossetti, 'Memoir', in *The Poetical Works of Christina Georgina Rossetti* (London: Macmillan, 1904), p. liii. 'She must no doubt have probed his faith and found it either strictly wrong or woefully defective.' Cf. B. S. Flowers, 'Introduction', in *Christina Rossetti: The Complete Poems*, text by R. W. Crump (Harmondsworth: Penguin, 2001), p. xliii.

3. See for example L. M. Packer, *Christina Rossetti* (Berkeley, CA: University of California Press, 1963).

4. 'Memoir', p. l. He describes her from this time onwards as 'an almost constant and often a sadly-smitten invalid'. Cf. Flowers, 'Introduction', p. xxxix.

5. A. H. Harrison, *Victorian Poets and the Politics of Culture. Discourse and Ideology* (Charlottesville: University Press of Virginia, 1998), p. 126; he describes her reputation as 'a saintly, reclusive author'. See also A. Leighton, 'Christina Rossetti', in *Victorian Women Poets: Writing Against the Heart* (London: Harvester Wheatsheaf, 1992), p. 122. She here refers to the well-known 'myth' of Rossetti as a 'saintly recluse'; whilst recognizing that this was not an accurate portrayal of the poet, Leighton argues that to some extent it was self-perpetuated.

6. See the examples given by Harrison, *Victorian Poets*, pp. 126–7, including the following obituary: 'Her language was always that of Christian assurance and of simple … faith in her Saviour … her life was one of transcendent humility.'

7. See A. Leighton, 'Christina Rossetti', p. 159 on Rossetti's doubts; also W. Rossetti, 'Memoir', p. lv. where he describes his sister as 'shadowed by an awful uncertainty'. Note further B. Horne, 'Poetry, English', in R. J. Coggins and J. L. Houlden (eds.), *A Dictionary of*

Biblical Interpretation (London: SCM, 1990), p. 552, who identifies a 'typical Victorian scepticism, even in those who seem to be believers'.

8. The high incidence of Eccl. 1.2 in nineteenth-century literature is particularly noteworthy: see for example, Browning's 'The Bishop Orders His Tomb at Saint Praxed's Church' (1845); Thackeray's *Vanity Fair* (1847); Melville's *Moby Dick* (1851) and Hardy's *Tess of the D'Urbervilles* (1891).

9. J. J. McGann, 'The Religious Poetry of Christina Rossetti', *Critical Inquiry*, 10 (1983), p. 130.

10. G. B. Tennyson, *Victorian Devotional Poetry. The Tractarian Mode* (Cambridge, MA: Harvard University Press, 1981), p. 45.

11. McGann, 'Religious Poetry', p. 132. He develops here an idea introduced by John O. Waller in his essay, 'Christ's Second Coming: Christina Rossetti and the Premillenarianist William Dodsworth', *Bulletin of the New York Public Library*, 73 (1969), pp. 465–82.

12. McGann 'Religious Poetry', p. 135.

13. McGann, 'Religious Poetry', p. 139.

14. D. Jasper, *The Study of Literature and Religion* (London: Macmillan, 1989), p. 7.

15. See for example N. Jiménez, *The Bible and Poetry of Christina Rossetti. A Concordance* (Westport, Connecticut: Greenwood Press, 1979), pp. vii–ix; D. Rosenblum, 'Christina Rossetti's Religious Poetry: Watching, Looking, Keeping Vigil', in A. Leighton (ed.), *Victorian Women Poets: A Critical Reader* (Oxford: Blackwell, 1996), p. 115; D. D'Amico, *Christina Rossetti: Faith, Gender and Time* (Baton Rouge: Louisiana State University Press), pp. 25–30; Flowers, 'Introduction', p. xl.

16. Jiménez, *Bible and Poetry*.

17. J. J. McGann, 'Christina Rossetti's Poems', in Leighton, *Victorian Women Poets*, p. 97.

18. C. D. Ginsburg, *Coheleth, Commonly Called the Book of Ecclesiastes* (London: Longman, Green, Longman, and Roberts, 1861), pp. 9–16 and pp. 244–55. Further details are provided in his extensive historical sketch of the exegesis of Ecclesiastes, pp. 213–43.

19. Ginsburg, *Coheleth*, p. 27. This view still prevails at the end of the twentieth century; see R. N. Whybray, *Ecclesiastes* (Sheffield: JSOT Press, 1989), p. 12: 'From the very first his readers have been unable to agree about his [Qoheleth's] basic attitude towards life … Two

thousand years of interpretation have utterly failed to solve the enigma.'

20. Ginsburg, *Coheleth*, p. 19; for a similar interpretation see also p. 78. Ginsburg provides a very useful summary of the variety of views circulating about Ecclesiastes in the nineteenth century, highlighting in particular the popularity of the book.

21. A list of the poems in which Rossetti uses Ecclesiastes can be found in Jiménez, *Bible and Poetry*, pp. 30–5. It is worth noting the Ecclesiastes passages that she employs, as she is highly selective. She quotes Eccl. 1.2, 1.6, 1.7, 1.8, 1.9, 1.14, 2.1, 2.2, 2.4, 2.22–3, 3.1, 3.15, 4.7, 6.10, 8.15, 9.10, 9.11, 11.7, 12.6.

22. See Rossetti's comments on the verse in her devotional work *Seek and Find* (London: SPCK, 1879), p. 272. She writes that Eccl. 1.2 'amounts to so exquisite a dirge over dead hope and paralysed effort that we are almost ready to fall in love with our own desolation; and seeing that "man walketh in a vain shadow" (Psalm 39.6, prayer-book version) to become vain as that shadow, and to drift through life without disquietude, because without either aim or aspiration'.

23. See for example William Dunbar's fifteenth-century poem 'Of the World is Vanitie'. The frequent use of Eccl. 1.2 in nineteenth-century literature is particularly striking: see note 8 above. For further occurrences of the phrase in literature see D. L. Jeffrey, *A Dictionary of Biblical Tradition in English Literature* (Grand Rapids, Michigan: Eerdmans, 1992), p. 807.

24. 'One Certainty', 'A Testimony', 'Sleep at Sea', 'Vanity of Vanities' (Ah woe), 'The Lowest Room', 'Mother Country', 'Saints and Angels', 'Maiden May', 'In the Willow Shade', 'Soeur Louise', 'If Thou Sayest', 'If love is not', 'Vanity of Vanities' (Of all the downfalls), 'O forza'.

25. McGann, 'Christina Rossetti', p. 112.

26. McGann, 'Christina Rossetti', p. 98.

27. All poems quoted are taken from the Penguin Classic edition, *Christina Rossetti: The Complete Poems*, text by R. W. Crump (Harmondsworth: Penguin, 2001).

28. Note here D'Amico, *Christina Rossetti*, p. 26. She argues that by using the first-person pronoun in the poem, Rossetti is associating herself with the Preacher; the true identity of the speaker is only

revealed in the final stanza. A similar point is made by C. Scheinberg, 'Victorian Poetry and Religious Diversity', in J. Bristow (ed.), *The Cambridge Companion to Victorian Poetry* (Cambridge: CUP, 2000), p.170. 'Rossetti claims an exegetical authority that is often denied to women.'

29. Eccl. 2.2 and 4.7. Further references to other parts of Ecclesiastes (1.7, 1.8, 2.4, 2.11) are made elsewhere in the poem.

30. See for example the work of J. D. Crossan, *The Historical Jesus: The Life of a Mediterranean Jewish Peasant* (Edinburgh: T. & T. Clark, 1991).

31. Cf. C. Cantalupo, 'Christina Rossetti: The Devotional Poet and the Rejection of Romantic Nature', in D. A. Kent (ed.), *The Achievement of Christina Rossetti* (Ithaca and London: Cornell University Press, 1987), p. 287.

32. Jiménez, *Bible and Poetry*, p. xi.

33. See McGann, 'Religious Poetry', p. 137 and 'Christina Rossetti', p. 103. Cf. also Harrison, *Victorian Poets*, p. 125. He notes that Rossetti wrote from 'a genuinely marginalized ideological position, that is, a position fundamentally opposed to the moral, economic, and political values that effectively dominated her culture'.

34. McGann, 'Christina Rossetti', p. 107.

35. Emphasis added.

36. See for example 'Up-Hill'.

37. The contrast between Rossetti and academic views in the mid-nineteenth century is here apparent. See Ginsburg, *Coheleth*, p. 228 where he comments that 'there are but few who can muster courage to defend Solomonic authorship'.

38. On the encouragement to enjoy the world in Ecclesiastes, see Eccl. 3.12. Note also the various summaries of the book's message which emphasize this dimension, for example A. Schoors, 'Ecclesiastes', in W. R. Farmer (ed.) *International Bible Commentary* (Collegeville, Minnesota: Liturgical Press, 1998), p. 884. 'A human being lives only once today; there is no morrow. Life is fixed in the laws of the world, in the inevitable, it is impossible to speak about future or hope. Therefore his practical advice is to enjoy life, for that joy is the gift of God.'

39. On death as a Victorian theme see B. Spurr, 'Victorianism – Faith and Doubt', in *Studying Poetry* (Basingstoke: Macmillan, 1997), p. 208; on Rossetti's ill-health see note 4 above.

40. See Leighton, 'Christina Rossetti', p. 159; McGann, 'Religious Poetry', p. 139; K. Alkalay-Gut, 'Aesthetic and Decadent Poetry', in J. Bristow (ed.), *The Cambridge Companion to Victorian Poetry* (Cambridge: CUP, 2000), p. 237.

41. For a short summary of Bradstreet's context see M. Drabble, *The Oxford Companion to English Literature* (Oxford: Oxford University Press, 2000), p. 878.

42. R. Atwan and L. Wieder, *Chapters into Verse. Poetry in English Inspired by The Bible* (Oxford: Oxford University Press, 1993), pp. 352–4.

43. Here Bradstreet appears to be drawing on the Lukan parable (Lk. 12.16–21).

44. McGann, 'Religious Poetry', p. 132.

45. P. S. Fiddes, *Freedom and Limit. A Dialogue between Literature and Christian Doctrine* (Basingstoke: Macmillan, 1991), p. 6.

46. S. Prickett, 'Biblical and Literary Criticism: A History of Interaction', in D. Jasper and S. Prickett (eds.), *The Bible and Literature. A Reader* (Oxford: Blackwell, 1999), p. 39.

Codifiability, Moral Wisdom, and the Foot/Hursthouse Thesis

Stephen J. Boulter

'I said, "I will be wise"; but it was far from me. That which is, is
far off, and deep, very deep; who can find it out?'
(Ecclesiastes 7.23–4)

In this chapter I explore some consequences of the view that normative
ethical judgements are not 'codifiable', and that the virtue theorist is correct
to restore moral wisdom to its rightful place at the heart of moral reflection.
The first such consequence is that the virtue theorist is open to the charge
of moral elitism in a form many are likely to find alarming. This charge
can be countered with what I call the Foot/Hursthouse thesis concerning
the egalitarian nature of moral wisdom, a thesis Hursthouse claims is 'an
assumption of virtue ethics'. However, I argue that the Foot/Hursthouse
thesis is untenable; indeed it is no more than a pious hope. A second, and
perhaps more surprising, consequence of the rejection of codifiability is
that the neo-Aristotelian virtue theorist will have to admit that human
free agency is far more restricted and precarious than is commonly assumed.
Indeed, if a form of moral elitism is not accepted our freedom may be so
restricted that the meaningfulness of moral discourse itself may be
threatened. If this is so, the fall of the codifiability assumption may
ultimately prove to be a pyrrhic victory for virtue ethics.

I

The emergence of virtue ethics as a credible alternative to both
consequentialism and deontology has provided one of the most important
challenges to philosophical reflection on moral matters witnessed in the

last quarter of the twentieth century. Its challenge occurs at at least two distinct levels. First, we are asked to re-evaluate our theoretical approach to moral problems, to break with intellectual habits engrained in us by our adherence to forms of consequentialism or deontology. Perhaps the most important theoretical challenge is the rejection of codifiability, a notion to be discussed more fully below. But the rejection of this theoretical assumption is not without consequences at a more profound level; for virtue ethics challenges some deep pre-theoretical moral intuitions,[1] the very 'data' of what Frank Jackson has charmingly called our 'folk morality'.[2]

One such intuition is that moral excellence is open to everyone equally. Moral excellence, it is usually assumed, is open to those from all social backgrounds, all genders, all age groups, and, most importantly for our present purposes, to the simple and unsophisticated as well as the intelligent and learned. Part of the rationale for this belief is the assumption that no special non-moral qualifications are required in order to be a morally excellent human being. This moral egalitarianism, as we might call it, appears to be a corollary of the distinctly Christian assumption that 'being good' is largely, if not entirely, a matter of the will. The overriding importance accorded to the will in moral matters is nicely expressed in Augustine's dictum, 'Love, and do as thou wilt.'[3]

But if the virtue theorist is to be believed, this egalitarian picture captures at best half the story of our moral situation. For the fundamental insight at the heart of virtue ethics is that, *pace* Augustine, lighting upon the (or a) correct course of action in a given situation is often exceedingly difficult, requiring much wisdom and experience and possibly even information not available to all and sundry. In sum, the will to do good is often not enough. When expressed explicitly in this fashion this 'insight' will strike some as a fairly obvious point, perhaps even platitudinous. For who among us has not encountered difficult moral situations? Indeed, applied ethics is full of precisely such examples of real moral quandary. But if this is so the immediate implication, often going unnoticed, is that it is highly unlikely that moral excellence will be open to everyone equally. For if we fail to act as we should, it is not necessarily a failing of the will that is to blame. It may be that, lacking the requisite intellectual sophistication, we simply do not know what a particular situation demands of us. And as I shall argue below, when we act through ignorance the will is not properly engaged at all.[4]

The question I wish to examine here, a question ultimately forced upon us by the rejection of codifiability, is whether moral excellence and moral wisdom require a degree of intellectual sophistication not attainable by all. Philippa Foot and Rosalind Hursthouse, prominent and highly respected proponents of virtue ethics, think not. Hursthouse takes it to be an assumption of virtue ethics that 'the sort of wisdom that the fully virtuous person has is not supposed to be recondite; it does not call for fancy philosophical sophistication, and it does not depend upon, let alone wait upon, the discoveries of academic philosophers'.[5] In this she is following Foot, who writes:

> There belongs to wisdom only that part of knowledge which is within the reach of any ordinary adult human being: knowledge that can be acquired only by someone who is clever or who has access to special training is not counted as part of wisdom, and would not be so counted even if it could serve the ends that wisdom serves ... Some people are wise without being at all clever or well informed: they make good decisions and they know, as we say, 'what's what'.[6]

This is the nub of what I shall call the Foot/Hursthouse thesis.

Despite the deserved eminence of both Foot and Hursthouse, I will argue here that moral excellence does in fact require intellectual sophistication, and that it is to the credit of virtue ethics that it can accommodate this, perhaps unwelcome, fact of life.[7] This view will not be warmly received by many given the dim view taken of most forms of elitism in our egalitarian times. But it is perhaps best to acknowledge that this is potentially a particularly offensive form of elitism. Most are willing to recognize that human beings come in a range of shapes, sizes and colours, and with varying degrees of talent. But none of these admissions threatens the view that human beings are fundamentally of equal value. Things are not so clear cut when degrees of moral achievement are mooted. It is hard to resist the feeling that one's worth as a person is on the line in such contexts. If I am right though, such a conclusion follows hard on the heels of the rejection of the codifiability assumption.

However, I will go on to argue that elitism in the form presented here is the least of the virtue theorist's worries. Not because this form of elitism is in fact more in tune with our 'folk morality' than we might care to admit. (Our egalitarianism is only skin deep.) Nor because the consequences of moral elitism may not be as nasty as first imagined. Paradoxically, in our current egalitarian climate moral humility is not a common commodity precisely because there is an in-built hostility to the idea of moral authorities. The worry I have in mind is that to reject codifiability (as I believe we must) *and* the elitism I propose, threatens the very meaningfulness of moral discourse by undermining one of its essential preconditions: the fact that we are, at least on occasion, free and responsible agents. Such a result is in fact more at odds with 'folk morality' than the elitism it sought to avoid.

A good deal of scene-setting is required in order to make this case at all plausible. Some clarification of the phrases 'moral excellence' and 'intellectual sophistication' is needed, as is some discussion of the nature of *phronesis*, translated into Latin as *prudentia*, and into English as 'practical or moral wisdom'. A brief account of Aristotle's understanding of voluntary action is also in order. Thankfully most of this can be kept to a minimum, and, if I am right, will amount to no more than a collection of reminders of more or less obvious points. But I start with an account of the developments in current moral philosophy which have brought us to our present impasse. This account will serve two purposes. First, it will motivate our current discussion. Second, it will become clear that virtue theorists of some repute have not included the Foot/Hursthouse thesis amongst their working assumptions while remaining virtue theorists for all that.

II

One of the most notable recent developments in moral philosophy has been the increasing recognition of the importance of what is best described as moral or practical wisdom.[8] This long-neglected notion has returned to view because of increasing scepticism concerning a common assumption underlying both consequentialism and deontology, an assumption adopted from natural law theory. Until relatively recently it has been a commonplace that the task of any adequate normative theory is to put forward and defend a 'codifiable' set of universal rules or principles with two particular features: (a) the rules or principles are to provide a decision procedure that allows one to determine what action is required in any particular set of circumstances; and (b) the rules or principles are to be stated in language that anyone and everyone can understand and apply, even those lacking the moral virtues.[9] Utilitarianism provides a particularly clear example of this approach to normative theory. It identifies one basic principle of moral action (one ought to act in such a way as to increase the overall amount of happiness – pleasure, satisfaction of preferences, or whatever – for all affected by the proposed action), and it is assumed, plausibly, that the language of pleasure, or of preferences, is transparent to all.

This understanding of the task of normative theory is no longer as secure as it once was. If the proof of any theoretical approach is in the pudding, then this approach to normative ethics has decidedly failed, since no such set of rules and principles has been identified. It has become increasingly clear that abstract principles, of any normative flavour, do not provide the sought-after methodical decision procedure when once we descend into the messy and often complex cases encountered in real life. Having mastered an abstract theory is simply no guarantee that one will know what to do in real life circumstances because rules and principles do not apply themselves. As Hursthouse points out, it is now suspected that 'a certain amount of virtue and corresponding moral or practical wisdom (phronesis) might be required both to interpret the rules and to determine *which* rule was most appropriately to be applied in a particular case'.[10] Practical wisdom, judgement and perception, which involve a particular sensitivity to the morally salient facts of a given situation, are required in order to know how rules and principles are to be applied in particular cases. But according to virtue ethics such wisdom cannot itself be captured in a list of rules or principles. Hursthouse continues, 'The rejection of codification, I take it, involves ... the recognition that, whatever they may be, [rules and principles] provide very little in the way of general action-guidance, certainly not a code in accordance with which one can live and act well.'[11] McDowell echoes these sentiments, saying:

> If one attempted to reduce one's conception of what virtue requires to a set of rules, then, however subtle and thoughtful one was in drawing up the code, cases would inevitably turn up in which a mechanical application of the rules would strike one as wrong – and not necessarily because one has changed one's mind; rather, *one's mind on the matter was not susceptible of capture in any universal formula.*[12]

It is this recognition of the untenability of the codifiability assumption that has led to the current revival of interest in moral wisdom amongst normative theorists. For many this has meant a return to the ancient Greeks, particularly Aristotle, for whom the intellectual virtue or excellence of practical wisdom (*phronesis*) is arguably the *sine qua non* of moral virtue. He claims, 'it is impossible to be good in the full sense without practical wisdom'.[13] And he insists that 'with the presence of the one quality, practical wisdom, will be given all the virtues'.[14] According to Aristotle no other virtue, including the moral virtues, is possible without practical wisdom because all virtues involve the application of practical reasoning.[15]

I believe that the return of *phronesis* to centre stage of ethical thinking is to be welcomed as part of a more realistic account of our moral lives, particularly given our failure to codify ethics; but the consequences of its rediscovery have yet to be fully explored. We have reason to believe, I think, that these consequences will be largely salutary if only because they shake us out of our overly optimistic belief that philosophical reflection could somehow provide simple answers to difficult questions.

But being disabused of this overly optimistic belief forces us to recognize the importance of the intellect in moral matters, and this is not without its darker consequences. For the spectre of elitism now forces itself upon us on account of the undeniable fact that the intellectual virtues, including *phronesis*, are not distributed equally. This development will strike some as pernicious. Consider, for example, the response now available to the oft-repeated point concerning the relativity of moral values and judgements. The less careful among us have often inferred that moral judgements cannot be objectively grounded in matters of fact given the undeniable existence of moral disagreement. Sextus Empiricus is certainly not the only person to make this move, but he is particularly frank and open about it. He writes, 'If things which move by nature move all men alike, while we are not alike moved by so-called goods, there is nothing good by nature.'[16] We might gloss Sextus's argument in the language of our contemporaries as follows: "Since there is moral disagreement about X, there cannot be any moral facts about X. And since there are no facts of the matter, moral values and judgements are simply an expression of one's subjective opinion." Our contemporary will then continue: "So you cannot tell me that I am wrong in my opinion about X, for there is no right and wrong about such matters, and any attempt to coerce me to adopt your view or to impose it upon me is simply an abuse of power." Now the assumption behind this argument is that all human beings are equally sensitive to the morally pertinent features of our lived experience, and so we must be deemed equally competent as judges in the moral arena. If we fail to agree, it is because there are no real facts our judgements are tracking.

But the response now available to virtue theorists is to deny these egalitarian assumptions. The virtue theorist will claim that there is no reason to believe *a priori* that we are all equally competent judges of morally complex situations. Some may simply be better moral judges than others, in the same way that some have better vision or hearing. In other words, the virtue theorist is willing to contemplate the possibility that moral disagreements stem from one or more of the disputants actually being in error. It is not that two incompatible but subjective opinions have been expressed; one of them may simply be false to the facts. As Iris Murdoch pointed out some years ago, '*Ignorance*, muddle, fear, wishful thinking, lack of tests often make us feel that moral choice is arbitrary, a matter for personal will rather than attentive study.'[17] Until this challenge from virtue ethics to current forms of non-cognitivism is soundly refuted, the hackneyed move from the variability of moral judgements to the denial of an objective moral realm will have lost even its rhetorical value.[18]

This line of argument is likely to alarm the supporters of multiculturalism and pluralism in general, not to mention feminists and other groups who feel marginalized by a society still largely dominated by white male Europeans. "Are we not striving to raise levels of tolerance and mutual respect between peoples of significantly different cultural, religious, social, and sexual persuasions?" it will be asked. "Is this talk of 'moral wisdom' not a barefaced attempt to claim for certain individuals or groups moral expertise that is denied to others? Is this not the high road to intolerance and bigotry?" Schneewind suggests that it is precisely these sorts of concerns that led to the decline in the fortunes of virtue ethics and which gave impetus to the search for moral rules and the hope of codifiability. He writes, 'The Aristotelian theory may have been suited to a society in which there was a recognized class of superior citizens, whose judgement on moral issues would be accepted without question. But the Grotians did not believe they lived in such a world.'[19] Nor, it should be said, do we. But at issue is whether we, along with the Grotians, are right.

The upshot of this brief history is that Aristotelian-based virtue ethics does not rule out the suggestion that excellence of character and moral judgement is impossible without a degree of intellectual sophistication. In fact some go out of their way to state the opposite. Consider these lines from Aquinas, one of the great authorities of the virtue ethics tradition:[20]

There are some cases in human action that are so explicit that they can be approved or condemned at once, with very little thought, by reference to … general and primary principles. Then, there are other problems for the judgements of which a good deal of thinking on the different circumstances is required. *Careful consideration of such problems is not the prerogative of just any person but of the wise.*[21]

In difficult cases *'the less favoured people are taught by those who are wise'.*[22] No pretence to moral egalitarianism here it would seem.

III

Let us now turn our attention to the clarification of certain key expressions. To begin with, what is meant by the expression 'moral excellence'? I cannot explore this topic here in any detailed way. I will simply state, without much in the way of supporting argument, intuitions on these matters I believe enjoy widespread support amongst virtue theorists and which are likely to find a place in a reflective 'folk morality'.

1. It is uncontroversial to say that moral excellence requires more than the mere performance of 'the right actions', whatever they may be. Doing the right thing is insufficient for moral excellence because one might simply be doing what one is told, as in the case of small children, in which case it is no bad thing. But while such actions are an important initial step on the way to moral excellence, an agent acting from these reasons remains far short of the final mark. Moreover, one might do the right thing from a less than laudable motive, as when one saves a drowning man in the expectation of a reward. Saving the drowning man is in most cases the right thing to do, but when done from these motives we do not believe the agent has manifested moral excellence.

2. It is not enough, as Kant rightly points out, to perform an action because one is inclined to do so out of the goodness of one's heart. While good intentions and motives are valuable in and of themselves, they are not sufficient for moral excellence in the full sense. The reason for this is that good intentions do not provide the right sort of link between the agent and her good action. Human beings are extremely susceptible to self-deception, and our true motives are often hidden from us. Indeed, our declared good intentions may mask sinister motives. Moreover, it is a

commonplace that the road to hell is paved with good, kind, and sincere intentions. Many an inquisitor burned a heretic out of genuine concern for the latter's well-being, and many a meddler has been excused and condemned simultaneously with the words, "Don't be too hard on her, you know she means well." The upshot of this is that if right actions do happen to flow from good intentions this may be entirely by accident, for disastrous actions flow from good intentions as well. The fortuitous nature of the link between the intention behind an action and the rightness of the action itself is not the kind of connection we expect to find between a morally excellent agent and her actions. In short, kindly motives and inclinations, even when genuine, are not enough for moral excellence either.

3. For an agent to be morally excellent in the fullest sense, the right actions must be done for the right reasons and with the right emotional/ affective accompaniment (the right mood music). Aristotle says with regard to good actions that 'both the reasoning must be true and the desire right, and the latter must pursue just what the former asserts'.[23] The importance of the right reasoning is emphasized when Hursthouse herself points out that a fundamental precept of virtue ethics is that one cannot have the right attitude to things if the attitude is based on or involves false beliefs.[24] But the essential point for present purposes is that one must know what one is about in order to qualify as having acted virtuously in the fullest sense of the word. To take an example from outside virtue ethics, according to deontological theories the right action to perform in any given situation is one sanctioned by a set of moral rules. Now someone might be able to tell that an action is in accordance with a set of moral rules. But the morally excellent person knows not just that a certain action is sanctioned by a set of rules, but also why those rules ought to be respected in the first place.

4. Finally, as Aquinas has already been seen to point out above, moral questions come in degrees of difficulty and complexity. Some moral matters are so straightforward that anyone with a basic moral competence can arrive at the right course of action. Others are not so easy, requiring greater moral perception and skill. The immediate consequence of this fact for our present purposes is clear enough: one is not thought to possess moral wisdom and excellence because one is able to recognize that, to take a particularly clear example, torturing babies for pleasure is not to be done. The 'not-to-be-doneness' of child abuse, or of killing people for fun, is easily and straightforwardly appreciated by all except the morally

retarded. The morally wise person, by contrast, is able to deal with difficult and complex cases: difficult because they may touch on issues about which no real consensus has yet been reached (for example, abortion, capital punishment, animal rights); complex because, in the messiness of real life, myriad competing interests have to be acknowledged and balanced. The morally wise person will know, for example, whether and when one's calling in the fields of art, politics, scholarship or whatever should be placed above the needs of one's family; or whether and when an unhappy relationship should be saved for the sake of the children; or, to take an example from the political realm, what the appropriate response(s) to the events of 11 September, 2001 might be. It is these sorts of cases that distinguish the morally excellent from the merely competent. To sum up then: one is deemed morally excellent when one is able to do the right thing for the right reasons with the right attitude, even when faced with difficult moral circumstances.

So much for 'moral excellence', what of 'intellectual sophistication'? Intellectual sophistication has at least two distinct aspects, one of which is not mentioned by Hursthouse. The first aspect concerns knowledge of 'recondite' facts, theories or discoveries. And for the time being I will count as 'recondite' information or knowledge that one cannot reasonably expect a normal adult human being to acquire in the course of their daily lives without making a particular and perhaps sustained effort. On this definition what counts as recondite is relative to time and place. What is recondite at one stage in history, for example, will not be so counted at a later stage if that information has become more widely disseminated.

However, while knowledge of recondite facts and theories is a necessary condition for intellectual sophistication, it is not sufficient. A second important aspect of intellectual sophistication concerns the cognitive skills and habits acquired and developed during one's training for a lifetime devoted to scholarly activity, to the 'life of the mind' as we are wont to call it. For intellectual sophistication is shown most clearly in one's *handling* of facts and theories, in one's being able to do something with the information one has. This aspect of intellectual sophistication is as much a matter of 'knowing how' as 'knowing that'. One such cognitive skill is the ability to distinguish between what is relevant in any given situation on the one hand, and irrelevant or at best tangential side issues on the other. (This skill can be developed, but it is difficult to instil.) Moreover, one's powers of concentration are increased significantly by a lifetime's habit of serious study. Put together, these skills make it less likely that the attention of the intellectually sophisticated person will be distracted from the relevant aspects of a given situation. As Aquinas once warned, 'If you don't use your mental dispositions, irrelevant and misleading images spring to mind which, if not cut down and kept in check, will weaken your skill in making right judgements.'[25]

The point for our present purposes is that knowledge of the latest intellectual discoveries or fashions is only one respect in which the learned are at an advantage *vis-à-vis* the less lettered. We should not lose sight of the fact that discoveries come and, in philosophy at least, most often go. The virtues of a trained mind are not so ephemeral.

IV

We can now turn to our main question: do moral excellence and moral wisdom require a degree of intellectual sophistication not attainable by all? We have already noted that Foot and Hursthouse maintain they do not. But no sooner is the thesis stated than they appear to backtrack, betraying a crisis of confidence. First, Foot admits that the egalitarian notion of wisdom is not that of Aristotle, for he explicitly states that practical wisdom (*phronesis*) is an intellectual, not a moral virtue. And it is clear that Foot's notion of wisdom is forced, at least in part, by her desire to uphold the thesis that virtues are matters of the will. Again this is not the view taken by Aristotle, who spends much time delineating the various intellectual virtues.

But Foot casts further doubt upon her thesis. She writes:

> [That] part of wisdom which has to do with values, is much harder to describe, because here we meet ideas which are curiously elusive, such as the thought that some pursuits are more worthwhile than others, and some matters trivial and some important in human life. Since it makes good sense to say that most men waste a lot of their lives in ardent pursuit of what is trivial and unimportant, it is not possible to explain the important and the trivial in terms of the amount of attention given to different subjects by the average man.[26]

Here Foot appears to acknowledge what most would accept, namely that wisdom is *not* manifested in the lives of 'the average man' in the street. This is by no means a new insight. Cicero lamented long ago that 'Our lives … are spent not with men who are perfect and manifestly wise, but with people who at best embody some pale reflection of virtue.'[27] And since Foot does not subscribe to the decidedly un-Aristotelian doctrine of original sin, this failure cannot be explained entirely by mass failures of the will.

What is more, Hursthouse openly admits she has no defence of the egalitarian thesis, and none has appeared in her latest book length discussion of virtue ethics. Indeed she writes, 'although most moral philosophers would be chary of claiming that intellectual sophistication is a necessary condition of moral wisdom or virtue, most of us, from Plato onwards, tend to write as if this were so'.[28] She also says that 'Sorting out which claims about moral knowledge are committed to this kind of elitism and which can, albeit with difficulty, be reconciled with the idea that moral knowledge can be acquired by anyone who really wants it would be a major task.'[29] She thereby at least tacitly acknowledges that *some* moral knowledge claims are committed to elitism.

These retractions suggest that the Foot/Hursthouse thesis is no more than a pious hope born of the desire to avoid the elitism which follows on the heels of the rejection of the codifiability assumption. This suggestion gains credibility when we consider more carefully what Aristotle has to say about *phronesis*. Again, no elaborate study is required, just a reminder of some of his key points. The burden of this section will be to make a case for the thesis that, no matter how much emphasis one wishes to put on the 'practical' in practical reasoning, its proper exercise presupposes recondite knowledge.

I begin with the observation that excellence of character is the willingness to act in whatever way practical reason requires. This claim is the heart of the Aristotelian doctrine. It makes it unambiguous that practical reasoning (*phronesis*) is fundamental to moral excellence. At issue is whether *phronesis, prudentia*, or practical wisdom, requires knowledge or cognitive skills that cannot be expected to be equally distributed amongst human beings.

Now it might be thought, after a quick reading of Aristotle's texts on the matter, that such knowledge and skills are not required since we are told that *phronesis* does not use philosophical wisdom but simply provides for its coming into being.[30] *Phronesis*, we are told, exercises knowledge of how to secure the ends of human life.[31] This line is supported by the claim that the function of practical reasoning is not to set goals but to choose the *means* of attaining pre-assigned goals. *Phronesis* is not about setting policy, a task preserved for 'political wisdom' (*politike*), but about the more down-to-earth problem of *implementing* policy. This workaday aspect of *phronesis* is captured by Hursthouse's quite homely definition of practical wisdom as 'the ability to reason correctly about practical matters'.[32] Aquinas says in a similar vein that *prudentia* is a disposition of reason to plan, judge and command right action.

But a little reflection reveals that this impression is mistaken. For Aristotle himself asks rhetorically about man's *telos* and the nature of *eudaimonia* (often translated as 'human flourishing' or 'well being'), 'Will not the knowledge of it have a great influence on life? Shall we not, like archers who have a mark to aim at, be more likely to hit upon what is right?'[33] The point here is that knowledge of the end of man, of the good life for man, must be included in the knowledge employed by practical wisdom.[34] As Aristotle himself points out, 'we credit men with practical wisdom in some particular respect when they have calculated well *with a view to some good end* which is one of those that are not the object of any art'.[35] In a similar vein, Foot insists that, while those possessing practical wisdom know the means to certain ends, they also know the worth of those ends and of human life in general.[36] If one does not know such things, then it is going to be very difficult to appreciate the morally salient features of any given situation. It is true that Hardie has argued that the man of practical wisdom need not know the ends of man, while such knowledge is essential to *politike*, or political wisdom. He says that having the virtue of practical wisdom 'does not involve the ability to formulate, or even perhaps fully to understand, the reasons for obeying the rules which are accepted [from politike]'.[37] But whatever the differences between practical wisdom and *politike*, they should not be exaggerated. After all, Aristotle himself states that they are 'the same state of mind'.[38] But even if *politike* and practical wisdom were significantly different in this respect, it is not unreasonable to think that those who *do* understand the ends of man would be in a better position to judge difficult cases.

The reason for objecting to Hardie on this point lies in the phrases that follow immediately upon a passage quoted above. Aristotle does say that, 'Phronesis does not use philosophical wisdom but provides for its coming into being.' But he goes on to say immediately that *phronesis* 'issues orders, then, *for its sake* but not to it'.[39] The implication here seems to be that one *does* need to know something of philosophical wisdom in order to issue orders effectively on its behalf, just as an archer must be able to see the target in order to shoot at it successfully. If one does not have this knowledge, one is reduced to the level of the foot soldier blindly following orders whose point in the wider picture is not revealed to him. The soldier kept on a 'need to know' basis is ineffectual once his situation fails to unfold as his superiors expect. Not knowing the wider significance of his orders, the point for which they were given in the first place, he does not know what is then required in his new circumstances. In fact he never knew why they were required at all. Such is the person who has a list of virtues to hand, but no clear conception of *eudaimonia*.

But the situation is even worse than this. For by common consent, one's conception of 'the good life for man' is *prior* to the concept of a virtue, the virtues being 'character traits one needs in order to flourish or live well'.[40] Moreover, one's conception of the virtues is itself prior to the correct employment of practical wisdom. One needs to know what the virtues are, and then possess them, in order to reason correctly about practical matters. The consequence of these conceptual dependencies is that *one will not know how to reason correctly about practical matters if one does not have a clear conception of 'the good life for man'*. But is it reasonable to say that such a conception is included in the average person's intellectual repertoire? Perhaps everyone, if forced, could state what they think makes for a good life. But not just any conception will do. Only *accurate* conceptions fit the bill. As Hursthouse puts it:

> Virtue is said to involve knowledge, and part of this knowledge consists in having the *right* attitude to things. 'Right' here does not just mean 'morally right', or 'proper' or 'nice' in the modern sense: it means 'accurate, true'. One cannot have the right or correct attitude to something if the attitude is based on or involves *false* beliefs.[41]

Now, is it at all plausible to say that the average person in the street has, not just 'a' conception of the good life, but an *accurate* conception of the good life? Once posed, does the question not answer itself? Perhaps more importantly we ought to ask: is it at all plausible to say that the average person in the street can acquire an accurate conception of the good life without making a sustained effort, and without straying into the arena of recondite knowledge? And let us be clear about the varieties of the 'can' in play here. Even if we thought that the average human being is capable of achieving such a conception of the good life (in the sense that they do not suffer from any intellectual handicaps) this is not enough for a true egalitarian. In the same sense that a legal right to X is pointless if one is not in a position to exercise that right, so the capability of achieving X is pointless unless one is given the circumstances in which that potentiality can be actualized. Do we believe that the average person in the street has the time, the energy, and the means required to engage in such a sustained effort?

It is perhaps worth pausing to illustrate the difficulties facing the average person in this regard in order to drive the point home. A particularly effective example is found in Hursthouse herself. She writes:

> One of Hume's most instructive mistakes is his conviction that he can dismiss 'celibacy, fasting and the other monkish virtues' without making any assumptions about 'the end of man'. Of course he cannot. He can dismiss them only if he assumes that human nature is as conceived by atheists and that thereby 'the end(s) of man' are given by ethical naturalism rather than supernaturalism.[42]

With this I entirely agree. But is it accurate to say that the average person in the street is well informed about the relative merits of these two metaphysically loaded conceptions of the ends of man? And what if we confine our attention to those conceptions that exclude mention of any supernatural ends of man? Clearly an existentialist's views of the nature of human beings, namely that there is no such nature, leads to a very different conception of the virtues than, say, that forwarded by an Aristotelian naturalist. Do we really think that the average person is in any position to pass judgement on the relative merits of these two conceptions of the ends of man? But if the foregoing argument is sound, the practically wise person will need to be able to make precisely these sorts of judgements.

This view is also made plausible by the fact that a correct conception of *eudaimonia* is precisely what would help the person of practical wisdom to make the right judgements in difficult cases. Consider these lines from John Austin's discussion of the 'machinery of action' in his 'A Plea for Excuses'. I choose this passage because it illustrates both the problem with the codifiability assumption, but also because, when read against the background of our discussion concerning the ends of man, it becomes clear just what it is in any given situation that we can fail to appreciate:

It happens to us, in military life, to be in receipt of excellent intelligence, to be also in self-conscious possession of excellent principles (the five golden rules for winning victories), and yet to hit upon a plan of action which leads to disaster. One way in which this can happen is through failure at the stage of *appreciation* of the situation, that is at the stage where we are required to cast our excellent intelligence into such a form, under such heads and with such weights attached, that our equally excellent principles can be brought to bear on it properly, in a way to yield the right answer. So too in real, or rather civilian, life, in moral or practical affairs, we can know the facts and yet look at them mistakenly or perversely, or not fully realize or appreciate something, or even be under a total misconception.[43]

Now it seems to me that an accurate conception of the ends of man, an accurate conception of *eudaimonia*, is precisely what one needs to know in order to 'cast our intelligence' into the required form, a form which enables us to see just what weight must be given to each feature of a given situation. But this is precisely what we cannot expect the average person in the street to possess.

V

The upshot of the foregoing section is that it is unreasonable to believe that moral wisdom and moral excellence are attainable by all, because both require a level of recondite knowledge and learning not available to all and sundry. One possible, and I would suggest, reasonable, response to this state of affairs is to accept an extension of the division of intellectual labour already in place in our society to include the moral realm. Much of what we think we know we do not know first hand, but only on the authority of experts. This is clearly the case with much modern science; perhaps we need to embrace a similar move in the moral realm.

Again some will baulk at the moral elitism implicit here, but this I believe is a mistake. For to deny this expertise to some because it is not available to all, or to reject the notion of moral knowledge itself as incoherent (and *a fortiori* moral experts) would be to break the conceptual connections between knowledge, action and responsibility.

To see the threat posed by the denial of elitism we must remind ourselves of what Aristotle had to say about the nature of voluntary action.

His approach to the voluntary is to begin at the opposite end as it were, that is, by considering when we think an action has been performed *in*voluntarily or *non*-voluntarily. (As Austin would say, it is the latter of this pair of concepts that 'wears the trousers'.) The operating assumption is to consider our normal actions to be voluntary (although it might be pointless or inappropriate to say so) unless there is a good reason to think they are not. Aristotle then says quite plausibly that 'Actions are regarded as involuntary when they are performed under compulsion or through ignorance.'[44] By marking out the territory of the involuntary, he provides a conceptual map of the voluntary as well. On Aristotle's account an act is voluntary if it meets two criteria. First, a voluntary act is one caused by the agent herself, that is to say one stemming from a principle (*archè*) within the agent. This criterion broadly marks the distinction between a self-determined act and one performed under coercion. The second criterion is that for an act to be voluntary the agent must carry out the act 'with knowledge of its end'.[45] As Aristotle says, 'Every act done through ignorance is non-voluntary, but it is involuntary when it causes the agent subsequent pain and repentance.'[46] He then lists a number of features of an action, ignorance concerning any one of which precludes the characterization of the act as voluntary. These are ignorance of (i) the agent, (ii) the act, (iii) the object or medium of the act, (iv) the instrument (e.g. the tool), (v) the aim, and (vi) the manner. It is feature (ii), ignorance of the act itself, which will demand attention in a moment.

But first, let us illustrate this understanding of the nature of voluntary action with a simple example. Consider the following circumstance: a hunter in the woods shoots and kills what in all honesty he takes to be a deer; but upon inspection, and to his horror, the deer turns out to be his father. Would we say that the hunter committed patricide? According to Aristotle, and I think according to common sense, we would have to say no. The hunter certainly caused the death of his father; but, and here's the point, it makes no sense to say that he did so voluntarily because he did not realize that that was what he was doing.

So to perform action X voluntarily one must know the nature of the act itself. And as Anscombe plausibly says, we can only say that an agent has acted knowingly, and therefore possibly voluntarily, if the action attributed to the agent is placed under a description the agent himself would recognize at the time of acting.[47] The crucial point for present purposes is that 'a man may know that he is doing a thing under one description, and not under another'.[48] Now I would submit that knowing the nature of an act involves knowing *more* than an accurate but purely non-moral description of the act. As Bostock points out, 'In practice we are going to be interested in that description … that is most relevant to the appraisal of the action as a good or bad thing to do.'[49] Indeed, I would suggest that an important part of knowing the nature of an act is to know which virtue or vice terms apply to it, for these terms supply the morally significant descriptions of the act, and it is these moral descriptions that concern us when ascribing praise or blame to agents.[50] The point of this scene-setting is to prepare the way for the claim that if we do not have a correct understanding of *eudaimonia*, then we are in fact ignorant of the nature of a significant number of our actions (feature ii), and in such cases do not act voluntarily.

This claim can be supported as follows: the primary role of practical and moral wisdom is the working out in daily life which courses of action are in line with the virtues. But, as noted above, the virtues and vices are determined by one's conception of *eudaimonia*, and so the description of one's possible actions, as falling under one virtue (or vice) concept or another, is determined by one's conception of *eudaimonia*. Consequently, if one has a mistaken conception of *eudaimonia*, then one's conception of the virtues will also be faulty. But if the conception of the virtues is faulty, then the deliverances of practical wisdom will themselves be faulty (or at best fortuitous shots in the dark) because they will involve faulty descriptions of the acts under consideration.

If this argument is sound, it is then reasonable to assume that if one acts through a faulty conception of *eudaimonia*, or without one at all, then one's *description* of one's actions will not match the description offered by, say, an ideal observer who is better placed to appreciate the true nature of your actions given their correct conception of *eudaimonia*. For example, what one could mistakenly describe as a courageous action under the influence of a faulty conception of *eudaimonia* might in fact be nothing but foolhardy bravado. But if the act is then performed under the faulty description, the agent is ignorant of the nature of the act itself, and so acts non-voluntarily (or involuntarily depending on their reaction to their mistake, should it ever be disclosed to them).

Now it seems to me that this argument can be extended to cover most of our morally significant actions, and so constitutes a serious threat to our status as free agents. This line of argument applies in many more cases than we might care to admit. But to suggest that no one ever acts voluntarily in morally significant situations, which is the consequence of saying that no one has a correct conception of *eudaimonia*, is not only counter-intuitive, it would undermine the very point of moral discourse. It would be far better to admit that *some* human beings do in fact have a substantially correct conception of *eudaimonia*, a conception that places them in a morally superior position to those who lack such a conception. The rest of us would then be in a position to profit from their wisdom, as we do already in the case of scientists and their expertise. More importantly, we would be in fact under an *obligation* to seek their counsel.[51] For if we choose *not* to profit from the wisdom of others, then our ignorance would no longer be innocent, and culpability would return to the agent.[52]

To sum up: it is only because the morally less expert among us have the possibility of consulting our wiser neighbours that most of us even count as moral agents at all. For if we do not have a correct conception of *eudaimonia* ourselves, and no possibility of consulting one who does, it makes little sense to say that we ever act voluntarily in morally significant situations.

VI

The fall of codifiability has boosted the prospects of virtue ethics at the expense of consequentialism and deontology. But before virtue theorists take too much comfort in this turn of events we must be clear about its consequences. Virtue ethics is likely to make demands on us we will not be able to wear comfortably, at least at first. Getting used to moral elitism is one such consequence. We need to be prepared to admit that non-moral qualifications are required for moral excellence. But perhaps the most pressing result for the virtue theorist is the full realization of the fact that the viability of virtue ethics depends upon the provision of a compelling and accurate conception of *eudaimonia*. Without such a conception the internal coherence of virtue ethics is compromised; even worse, virtue theorists will find it difficult to make room for a basic pre-condition of moral discourse, namely, human free agency. Such a conception must be found if the fall of codifiability is not to prove a pyrrhic victory for virtue ethics.

Notes

1. It is worth pointing out that virtue ethics' challenge to our gut moral intuitions stems in no small part from the fact that it returns to a tradition of moral philosophy well established before the advent of Christianity as a serious cultural force in the intellectual history of the West. For despite all the talk of the increasing secularization of modern society, our moral sensibilities, and much else besides, bear the unmistakable marks of our collective Christian, particularly post-Reformation, past. These Christian sensibilities are often at odds with the moral writings of the ancient Greeks, particularly Aristotle's *Nicomachean Ethics*, the seminal text of virtue theorists. Indeed, this mismatch of moral intuitions has often been a stumbling block to many, making it difficult for some to consider the *Nicomachean Ethics* as a work of ethics at all. See J. O. Urmson's work *Aristotle's Ethics* (Oxford: Basil Blackwell, 1988), where he identifies our Christian past as the first of 'the main sources of difficulty and misunderstanding in the reading of the *Nicomachean Ethics* not present in a typical modern philosophical text' (p. 4). For a historical account of some of these 'mismatches', see J. B. Schneewind's 'The Misfortunes of Virtue', in R. Crisp and M. Slote (eds.), *Virtue Ethics* (Oxford: Oxford University Press, 2000).

2. See chapter 5 of Frank Jackson's *From Metaphysics to Ethics: A Defence of Conceptual Analysis* (Oxford: Clarendon Press, 2000).

3. If we are honest with ourselves, so this story goes, we all know what we ought to do and how we ought to live. If we fail to achieve moral excellence it is because we simply cannot bring ourselves to do that which, at some level at least, we know ought to be done. St Paul captures this exactly when he confesses that 'The good I would do, that I do not, the evil I would not, that I do' (Rom. 7.19). The inevitable consequence of this attitude is a downgrading of the moral import of the intellect. This is reflected in C. S. Lewis's observation, placed in the mouth of the senior devil of *The Screwtape Letters*, that the great moralists of history do not provide new

information about moral matters, but simply *reminders* of what we all know but have conveniently forgotten or ignored. Even Christ's two 'new' commandments can be seen as merely 'summing up' the moral lessons present in the Old Testament.

4. This is not simply a restatement of the claims of the intellect in the age-old intellectualism vs. voluntarism debate. In fact no choice between the two is required for the purposes of this chapter. All that is required is the recognition that our failure to achieve or manifest moral excellence may be due to ignorance as well as to failures of the will.

5. 'Virtue Theory and Abortion', in Crisp and Slote, *Virtue Ethics*, p. 228.

6. 'Virtues and Vices', in Crisp and Slote, *Virtue Ethics*, p. 167. Hursthouse has clarified her position on this point in recent correspondence. While she remains an 'egalitarian' inasmuch as she does maintain that moral excellence does not require intellectual sophistication, she does nonetheless recognize that moral excellence is not open to everyone equally. However, her reasoning on this point has little to do with issues concerning intellectual ability and more to do with the quality of the moral education and training one receives as a child.

7. I think it goes without saying that intellectual sophistication is *not* a sufficient condition for moral excellence, but in order to avoid any possible misunderstanding it is worth making this explicit.

8. For work in this vein see in particular Hursthouse's *On Virtue Ethics* (Oxford: Oxford University Press, 1999). Much of this section is simply a paraphrase of relevant portions of this work as well as some points made in her previously published article, 'Virtue Theory and Abortion'.

9. This is a paraphrase of Hursthouse's account of what she calls 'codifiability' in *On Virtue Ethics*, pp. 39–40. In her article 'Virtue Theory and Abortion' she writes about the adequacy condition of any normative theory in more tendentious, but perhaps more revealing, terms: 'Any adequate action-guiding theory must make the difficult business of knowing what to do if one is to act well easy ... it must provide clear guidance about what ought to be done which any reasonably clever adolescent could follow if she chose.' (p. 224).

10. *On Virtue Ethics*, p. 40.

11. Ibid., p. 58.

12. 'Virtue and Reason', in Crisp and Slote, *Virtue Ethics*, p. 148. Emphasis added.

13. *Nicomachean Ethics*, trans. David Ross (Oxford: OUP, 1980), 1144b 22–23. Aquinas agrees with Aristotle on this point. He writes that 'Virtues are greater the nearer they approach the root of virtue in reason. Prudence perfects reason itself and is the source of goodness in the other moral virtues.' *Summa Theologiae*, I–II, q. 66, art. 1. He then arrives at the quite startling conclusion that 'the mental virtue of prudence is to be preferred to the moral virtues'. *Summa Theologiae*, I–II, q. 66, art. 7.

14. *Nicomachean Ethics*, 1145a 1. Admittedly this is a misleading statement of Aristotle's position. In fact Aristotle also goes out of his way to point out that 'it is impossible to be practically wise without being good'. *Nicomachean Ethics*, 1144a. His reasoning for this claim is extremely important. He argues that what is good for human beings presents itself as such 'only to the good man because vice perverts us and causes us to go wrong about principles of action'. But for the time being it is sufficient to note that practical wisdom is absolutely crucial to moral excellence.

15. Incidentally, it is this view of the central importance of practical wisdom that makes the hotly disputed thesis concerning the unity of the virtues at all plausible. If no virtue is possible without practical reasoning, then once these reasoning capacities have been acquired they ought to be applicable in all circumstances, making it reasonable to expect that if one has one of the virtues then it is likely that all virtues will be present at least to some degree. In this regard it is worth noticing that cognitive skills are commonly regarded as being the most 'transferable'.

16. *Outlines of Pyrrhonism*, III, trans. R. G. Bury (New York: Prometheus Books, 1990), p. 182.

17. 'The Sovereignty of Good over Other Concepts', in Crisp and Slote, *Virtue Ethics*, p. 109. Emphasis added.

18. Of course much more sophisticated arguments for non-cognitivism exist. But it is surprising how often the variability of moral judgements alone ('pluralism') is taken as support for non-cognitivism.

19. 'The Misfortunes of Virtue', in Crisp and Slote, *Virtue Ethics*, p. 200.

20. To reassure some readers on this point it might be worth quoting some remarks of Philippa Foot herself: 'It is possible to learn a great deal from Aquinas that one could not have got from Aristotle. It is my opinion that the *Summa Theologica* is one of the best sources we have for moral philosophy, and moreover that St Thomas' ethical writings are as useful to the atheist as to the Catholic or other Christian believer.' 'Virtues and Vice', p. 164.

21. *Summa Theologiae*, I–II, q. 100, a. 1. Emphasis added.

22. Ibid.

23. *Nicomachean Ethics*, 1139a 23–26.

24. 'Virtue Theory and Abortion', p. 228.

25. T. McDermott (ed.), *Summa Theologiae: A Concise Translation* (London: Methuen, 1991), p. 230, I–II, q. 53, a. 3. If anyone seriously doubts this I would suggest they spend an afternoon watching American daytime television, preferably the Rickie Lake Show. In the rarefied atmosphere of academe we run the risk of losing touch with the more 'popular' aspects of our society.

26. 'Virtues and Vices', pp. 167–8.

27. *On Obligations*, trans. P. G. Walsh (Oxford: Oxford University Press, 2001), p. 18.

28. 'Virtue Theory and Abortion', p. 228.

29. Ibid.

30. *Nicomachean Ethics*, 1145a 6–9.

31. 1140a 24 – 1140b 30.

32. *On Virtue Ethics*, p. 153.

33. *Nicomachean Ethics*, 1094a 22–24.

34. W. F. R. Hardie, *Aristotle's Ethical Theory* (Oxford: Clarendon Press, 1968), p. 224.

35. *Nicomachean Ethics*, 1140a 26–29.

36. 'Virtues and Vices', p. 167.

37. Hardie, *Aristotle's Ethical Theory*, p. 220.

38. *Nicomachean Ethics*, 1141b 23.

39. *Nicomachean Ethics*, 1145a 9–10.

40. Hursthouse, 'Virtue Theory and Abortion', p. 219.

41. Ibid., p. 228. Emphasis added.

42. *On Virtue Ethics*, pp. 242–3.

43. J. L. Austin, 'A Plea for Excuses', in *Philosophical Papers* (Oxford: Oxford University Press, 1979), p. 194.

44. *Nicomachean Ethics*, 1109b 35 – 1110a 36.

45. Aquinas, *Summa Theologiae*, I–II, q. 6, a. 1.

46. *Nicomachean Ethics*, 1110b 17–19.

47. 'To say that a man knows he is doing X is to give a description of what he is doing *under which* he knows it.' *Intention* (New York: Cornell University Press, 1966), p. 12.

48. Ibid., p. 11.

49. D. Bostock, *Aristotle's Ethics* (Oxford: Oxford University Press, 2000), p. 108.

50. If this point does not seem obvious consider the words of Christ upon the cross: "Forgive them Father, for they know not what they do" (Lk. 23.34). Obviously those crucifying Christ did know in some sense what they were doing. But they did not appreciate the moral significance of their actions, and so in a very important sense did not know what they were doing.

51. Aristotle quotes Hesiod with approval: 'Far best is he who knows all things himself; Good, he that hearkens when men counsel right; But he who neither knows, nor lays to heart Another's wisdom, is a useless weight.' *Nicomachean Ethics*, 1095b 10–13. These lines summarize the principal themes of this chapter.

52. I must defer a full discussion of the issue of culpable ignorance until another occasion.

'The Holy of Holies': Something Queer in Reformist Political Theology

Graeme Smith

In his seminal work, *Christianity and Social Order*, William Temple generated a theological vacuum, a space that the theologian *qua* theologian cannot enter.[1] Temple's analogy of the theologian and the civil engineer serves to make the point.[2] Nothing in the studies of theologians will equip them to construct a bridge; specialist civil engineering skills and knowledge are required for the task. The unwitting civil engineer may be the beneficiary of advice from the theologian, namely, ensure the bridge is safely constructed, but this is shouted from beyond the portals. Temple does not preclude a fortuitous symbiosis, in one person, of civil engineer and theologian but, when it comes to the construction of the bridge, the civil engineer not the theologian treads on holy ground. There is a 'holy of holies', a shrine in which the theologian may not trespass, the sacred space of the expert, the specialist. The theologian may speak of 'principles' and 'ends' but not of details, nor specifics; these are the province of the technician, be it engineer or politician.[3] Unless the theologian *qua* theologian will adopt the garb of the enthusiastic amateur then their knowledge and skills, their wisdom, is limited, and even then not theological.

A similar theological vacuum is generated in a different manner by Peter Hinchliff.[4] Hinchliff discerns the instruments of compromise, expediency and pragmatism as essential tools of the politicians' trade. He elects one of their number, David Owen, as representative and illustrator of the politicians' art. Owen presents, in a manner that will not be surprising to his political foes, a defence of the morality of compromise, based on expediency, over and against the exaltation of principle.[5] For Hinchliff morality cannot inhabit the same sphere as compromise, expediency or pragmatism; political morality is caught in a catch-22 scenario of being applicable only to principles that cannot find political expression without losing that which makes them principled and thereby moral.[6] There are two arenas: the principled arena of the ideal and the absolute, in which theologians are eloquent, even verbose, the debating chamber of politics, and the compromised arena of the expedient and pragmatic, the locus of decision making, the mysterious world of the ministerial office, a sacred space dimly visible to the theologian. Hinchliff struggles to square the (magic) circle of theological politics without infecting the purities of morality and theology with the dirty business of daily political realities.

Value-led Political Theology

Contemporary reformist political theology is characterized, almost universally, by an unwillingness to reflect theologically beyond the philosophical, the principled or the value-led.[7] For example, there have been critics of a dependence on specialists, but the focus of these theologians remains on more general values or principles. Duncan Forrester summons up Marxist theory to doubt the perspective of the expert.[8] His amalgam of liberation theology and Augustinianism envisages a new order of equality for the powerless, informing the political pilgrim in this age. The edifice of political life is supported by two pillars, vision and values, about which the theologian may speak but go no further. The moral worth of values may be made relative, as Forrester recognizes in the exegesis of Alasdair MacIntyre, but he remains a tenacious exponent of value-led political theology.[9] The political theologian offers free floating 'theological fragments', formed in the womb of Christian metanarrative but offered as mature, independent nuggets of wisdom capable of holding their own in the secular pluralism of postmodern society. The actual politician, maybe the actual political theologian, will apply these values to the world the theologian only sees dimly, the world of red boxes, working majorities, civil servants, preferment and party intrigues.

When it comes to reformist political theology focusing on a discussion of principles and values, Forrester is the rule rather than the exception. Henry Clark, in his analysis of these methodological matters in the Thatcher period, cites what he describes as the 'most audacious statement regarding the Church's social witness made during the period under consideration', namely *Living Faith in the City*.[10] The statement spoke of 'principles', philosophical shift', and 'underlying assumptions', meaning something similar to values and vision, as the locus of theological engagement with what Clark, amongst others, saw as the essential enemy: the government. James Gustafson, in his four-fold analysis of ecumenical social theology, draws a distinction between the prophetic mode of 'moral discourse' and 'policy discourse'.[11] The primary purpose of the prophetic is to inspire and motivate; however it is not informative when it comes to matters of policy, this requires a mediating set of 'ethical principles and human values'.[12] Policy discourse exists in social theological literature, but, 'much of this material simply repeats what was, and is, available to the reader of both technical scientific literature and policy literature of these matters'.[13] His conclusion is that 'It is not easy to justify a policy preference on moral or theological grounds.'[14]

Significantly the politicians seem only too eager to buttress this sacred space, the theological no-fly zone. Tony Blair, addressing the Christian Socialist Movement prior to the 2001 election, spoke not of compromise, expediency or pragmatism but of 'values'.[15] Of course we must permit Blair the right to be disingenuous, it is a significant weapon in the politician's arsenal, and so, although he does also speak of policy, and the implementation of policy, the shift from values to policy is seamless. Blair's faith, as far as it can be classified from public utterances, is essentially liberal: 'the equal worth of all citizens', 'individual responsibility', and 'the self best realised in community', although the descriptor he selects is Christian, or rather 'Multi-Faith Tolerant' of which he belongs to the Church element.[16] Blair allows us a little glimpse into his world by stating that 'policy is the business of politics. And it is not an easy business'; but then, as if to undermine his own point, with remarkable ease we glide · from 'individual responsibility' to 'New Deal, the minimum wage and the Working Families Tax Credit'.[17]

The question Blair's comments raise, following many others before him, is whether it is legitimate to propose a division between principles, values and philosophies, and compromise, expediency and pragmatism. Blair states, 'Politics without values is sheer pragmatism. Values without politics can be ineffective', the second sentence echoing David Owen's critique.[18] There are two conundrums: can we conceive of the pragmatist who is not, even unwillingly, enacting a vision through their activities; or the visionary who, as they beautify the contemporary with critical hope, is not enacting political strategy? In response, clearly vision might be interpreted as the future to which the consistent application of current activities inevitably leads, and it might be interpreted more idealistically. But this alone would not demonstrate the existence of only one space for politician and theologian to cohabit, if the theologian discusses only the vision and not the actual activities. It is also the case that the annunciation of values or vision, and political activity, are simultaneous events but this further illustrates the theologically neglected region, for what the theologian debates are the values and vision, whereas it is political strategy that is being enacted.

The Queer Silence of the Political Theologian

There is a silence on the part of the reformist political theologian when it comes to the ordinary business of political life, the politicians' routine, their consuming passion, what can be called the politicians' area of expertise. Reformist political theology holds a mirror up to the maelstrom of political activity, blanking out its detail and seeing in its stead visions of society, underlying philosophies, meanings, values and purposes, in fact its own existence. And like so many silences this one speaks volumes about its source. It alerts us to something amiss in this political theology, something strange in a discourse which speaks to its own reflection, in fact something queer, or at least something that could be made queer. Reformist political theology seems to have neutered its subjects; politicians are philosophical, ideological and theological billboards, without friends and allegiances, without desires and ambitions, no longer flattering, cajoling, or threatening. In fact political life hardly seems political at all, it resembles more closely the academy, or, perhaps more accurately, a fantasy academy devoid, of course, of academics.

The successful politician is not defined by, or more significantly created by, the critical resilience of their ideas, the coherence of their philosophy, or the self-evident truth of their proposals. A brief vignette demonstrates how political life is frequently interpreted by those who observe it without the lens of theology. Hugo Young writes of Margaret Thatcher, 'She was not an accomplished theoretician, and she never had an original idea … she dealt in simple convictions, which survived in some fashion even while, as a minister, she was doing and watching others do exactly the opposite of where those convictions ought to have pointed.'[19] Of her appointment of a new shadow chancellor once she became leader of the Conservative

Party Young comments, 'the obvious man for the job was Joseph, who had invented most of what she now believed in. But here the leader showed early wisdom, and some command of the capacity without which no leader survives for long – a talent for well-measured brutality. She left Joseph on the sidelines, with overall responsibility for policy and research [sic!] ... Howe had many qualifications for the post. But the first of these was again that he was a convert: the first and chief of converts. Only a year before he had been a central ally not of Joseph but of Heath.'[20] Of the appointment of deputy leader Young writes, 'The first of the loyalists to declare for her was William Whitelaw, who decided immediately after his defeat to accept an invitation to become her deputy leader. In time theirs became a rich relationship, with Whitelaw the key instrument for the neutering of her enemies', meaning enemies within the Conservative Party.[21] Of the construction of the shadow cabinet Young suggests, 'For the leader it was a question of distinguishing between those, the majority, whose public loyalty concealed a belief that any Thatcher revolution would not last, and those who could be trusted to support her.'[22]

Politics in this vein is characterized by compromise, expediency and pragmatism as well as alliance building, ambition, a certain ruthlessness, good fortune, opportunism, personal charisma, loyalty, friendship, desire for power and factionalism. This is not to condemn political life, in fact we could celebrate its rich, glorious humanity, but to describe what is absent in reformist political theology. Ideas are banished to the sidelines – the wilderness even (of policy and research) – by these vibrant, very personable people intent on competition and, ultimately, ministerial office. The wilderness is a location strenuously avoided by politicians but in which they are occasionally, maybe only once in their career, forced to find refuge, and where they might be recreated.[23]

Nor is intrigue the sole preserve of the Conservative Party. Alan Clark, an academically qualified Conservative, indiscreetly exhibits the place of intimate relations in political life with his devoted references to 'the Lady', and his admiration or scorn for many others.[24] What is voyeuristic in Clark becomes tragicomic with New Labour. Donald Macintyre reveals closet details of the New Labour 'family' at the time of Peter Mandelson's first resignation: 'Tears were shed by Mandelson, and briefly by Campbell, who hugged his old friend.'[25] Macintyre judges the events to be like a 'family bereavement', with the Blairs that night providing hospitality at Chequers for the chief mourner.[26]

Andrew Rawnsley, whose relationship with New Labour is warmer than Hugo Young's with Thatcherism, resorts to the most intimate of metaphors to describe the politics which dominate the current government. As it was reported to him, Blair suggested that 'his relationship with his Chancellor was like "a marriage"'.[27] It certainly sounds like a marriage, albeit a stormy one: 'Aides and colleagues remarked upon the extraordinary efforts Blair devoted to managing Brown. "He mediates, he negotiates, he defuses, he cajoles, he rails, he shouts, he hugs, he flatters," according to a close observer of the relationship.'[28] And as Rawnsley, Macintyre and John Rentoul note, the Blair–Brown relationship was but one at the heart of the New Labour nexus.[29]

Andrew Rawnsley is an award-winning journalist, as is Hugo Young, and both have editors to please and publishers to reward, so perhaps we have merely shifted from the puritanical, those whose gaze is averted from all but the ideological, down Fleet St. to the prurient who, again, merely hold a mirror to themselves, or their view of public interest, as they rummage for gossip and innuendo. Perhaps what is queer belongs to the journalists rather than the silence of the theologians. However, such thoughts are undone by the suppressed anger, but far from journalese, of John Major reflecting on his own, and New Labour's, experience of government. Of the former he notes that 'squabbling', 'spats', and 'squalls', did not 'trouble the combatants' (over Europe) who failed to perceive that 'the more they debated the minutiae of our policy in public, the slimmer our chances of being in office to carry it out became'.[30] In a more sombre tone he remembers that to experience government is to experience 'the choices, disappointments and mistakes that always take place. Since the election (of May 1997) they have come to experience some of the necessary compromises of office'.[31]

Personal Identity and Political Culture

None of the above should be taken to mean there is no place for values, visions or principles in political life, clearly there is. But often the head does not rule the heart; they work in tandem, so what you believe is not only the consequence of reflection and contemplation but also the fruit of alliances and friendships, the fulfilment of desires and ambitions, a product of accidental circumstance, in fact, a sense of our personal identity forged in a social and cultural milieu. Heather Walton analyses what has been made explicit by the politics of Blair and Thatcher, namely, political commitment is that most intimate and personal of things, a life-style choice.[32] What we believe to be true belongs to the same constellation as who are our friends, what satisfies our needs, what inspires and nurtures our drive and commitment. A group of former Communists employ religious language to explain this fusion of ideology and identity, in a collection of essays edited by Richard Crossman whose title is indicative, *The God that Failed*. Crossman draws parallels, seemingly without irony, between faith in Roman Catholicism and faith in Marxist ideology: one is converted to both.[33] It is necessary to go beyond reason if one is to challenge the adherent because any intellectual challenge 'involves a challenge to his fundamental faith, a struggle for his soul'.[34] The apostate Crossman explains this in terms that are theological, rather than cultural as employed by Walton, although they refer to the same phenomenon, 'for it is very much easier to lay the oblation of spiritual pride on the altar of world revolution than to snatch it back again'.[35]

The author Arthur Koestler shares Crossman's experience of the primacy of non-rational factors when it comes to the conversion of the ideological adherent. Political commitment is intently personal; 'Persuasion may play a part', he writes, 'but only the part of bringing to its full and conscious climax a process which has been maturing in regions where no persuasion can penetrate. A faith is not acquired; it grows like a tree.'[36] The horticultural metaphor is later repeated, 'I was ripe to be converted, as a result of my personal case-history.'[37] The consequence of conversion is a new hermeneutic, absorbed by the proselyte: 'Gradually I learned to distrust my mechanistic preoccupation with facts and to regard the world around me in the light of dialectical interpretation.'[38] The role of alliances and friendships is illustrated somewhat *in extremis* by the life of 'the cell', as described by Koestler, and, even more severely, by the trial described by Richard Wright. At the cell meetings Koestler attended, the Party handed down a 'line' on any given issue. This was discussed following the Communist hermeneutic, that is, as Koestler writes, 'We groped painfully in our minds not only to find justifications for the line laid down, but also to find traces of former thoughts which would prove to ourselves that we had always held the required opinion.'[39] It can also be the case that once a line was identified with the Communists, others sought, equally painfully, for reasons why these views should be rejected, something which can sound familiar and contemporary. The process led Koestler at the time to write a pamphlet explaining to the German working class why Japanese aggression against China was more important to them than high unemployment or the threat of fascism; further he writes, 'the pat on the shoulder I received for it from District HQ still makes me feel good – I can't help it'.[40]

Richard Wright portrays the events that led a Party member, Ross, to condemn himself at a Communist Party trial in Chicago. Wright describes the form of the meeting, 'an amazingly formal structure … a structure that went as deep as the desire of men to live together', something of a liturgy in fact.[41] It began with an analysis, following the norms of dialectical materialism, of the international situation and then the role of the Soviet Union as the only workers' State in world history. This led to a description of the situation in Chicago and especially the experience of Black people on the South Side. Wright reports how a momentum of indisputable facts was built up over a period of three hours, 'it had enthroned a new sense of reality in the hearts of those present'.[42] Finally the charges were brought against Ross, 'not by the leaders of the Party, but by Ross's friends, those who knew him best! It was crushing, Ross wilted. His emotions could not withstand the weight of the moral pressure'.[43] Wright states that no one was forced to accuse Ross, the comrades did so willingly:

> The moment came for Ross to defend himself. I had been told that he had arranged for friends to testify in his behalf, but he called upon no one. He stood, trembling; he tried to talk and his words would not come. The hall was as still as death. Guilt was written in every pore of his black skin. His hands shook. He held on to the edge of the table to keep on his feet. His personality, his sense of himself, had been obliterated. Yet he could not have been so humbled unless he had shared and accepted the vision that had crushed him, the common vision that bound us all together.
>
> "Comrades" he said in a low, charged voice, "I'm guilty of all the charges, all of them."
>
> His voice broke in a sob. No one prodded him. No one tortured him. No one threatened him. He was free to go out of the hall and never see another Communist. But he did not want to. He could not. The vision of a communal world had sunk down into his soul and it would never leave him until life left him. He talked on, outlining how he had erred, how he would reform.[44]

What causes a free man in a free society to submit to this misery? It is the strength of cultural identity, the interconnections of believing and belonging, the fusion of the public and the personal. And whilst this may be an exhibition at the extremities, the margins of political activity, it is nevertheless indicative. No one suggests this level of intensity is typical for the Thatcherite or Blairite; but nor can we suppose that the forces at work in Ross's trial are not operating, in diluted form, in all political commitment. The integration of liturgy and litany are features of political existence, a given of its operations, to be condemned in oppressive and absolute form and to be recognized universally.[45] What these Communists, and others, depended upon was the unity of values, principles and beliefs, with social networks, and with cultural identity, in other words an anthropology of the whole person.

A Theology of Compromise

The silence in reformist political theology becomes all the more queer when it is realized that the importance of personal relations in political life and political culture has previously been identified. Hugh Montefiore, writing from the perspective of a former Chair of the Church of England's Board of Social Responsibility and Bishop in the House of Lords, states that often personal contact with the appropriate government Minister can be more appropriate than a General Synod resolution.[46] Medhurst and Moyser recognize that Bishops can have a quiet word in the corridors of power, and that one aspect of the role of the Archbishop of Canterbury is to keep open channels of communication with the government of the day.[47] Moyser, in the same collection of essays, argues, albeit briefly, that the churches need to take account of contemporary political culture.[48]

Ray Plant, along with others, presents the silence as an ecclesiastical dilemma. The churches have to choose between general and vacuous statements on political matters and the divisive stratagem of joining the political debate by taking sides in party politics.[49] The dilemma is that division can lessen the authority of any ecclesiastical pronouncement. Others see this as the merging of an eternal and absolute Kingdom of God with a temporal and provisional political programme, something they cannot sanction.[50] Giles Ecclestone presses the ethical case for a study of the operations and realities of political life especially bearing in mind the attractions of single issue politics over against institutional, from his perspective, Westminster politics.[51] His plea is to a certain extent answered, and reinforced, by the Roman Catholic Bishops of England and Wales who, whilst promoting party political activity as a proper vocation, warn politicians not to bring their work into disrepute.[52] They state, 'It is not ignoble to want a successful political career, nor dishonourable for politicians to seek political power' however such an injunction depends on them taking their 'Catholic principles' with them and does not include detailed guidance on how to deal theologically with the issues of compromise, pragmatism and expediency outlined above.[53]

In one sense John Habgood, former Archbishop of York and thereby sometime wanderer amidst the corridors of power, belongs with this group who separate theological reflection from the art and practice of politics. His position is ambiguous, however, because he also develops ideas about the notion of compromise. Around the question of principles Habgood offers a slightly different analysis from many cited above, suggesting that Christians have little to say that cannot be said by people of 'goodwill'.[54] For Habgood the priority is not to comment on political or policy matters, the main business of theologians is to be theological:

> It is Christian belief about the kind of place the world is, about the depth of human sinfulness and the possibilities of divine grace, about judgement and hope, incarnation and salvation, God's concern for all and his care for each, about human freedom and divine purpose – it is beliefs such as these which make the difference, and provide the context within which the intractable realities of social and political life can be tackled with wisdom and integrity.[55]

Habgood could be read along the lines of Stanley Hauerwas, that is, suggesting that the churches' political theology stems from their counter-cultural witness as Church in society.[56] In the alternate community individuals are formed and resourced for a wise or virtuous discipleship within society, including politics. The formative significance of community and culture for belief and activity is recognized, meaning this theology might well be a response to the issue of reformist political theology's silence about political community and culture. It would not be the case that the daily business of politics was the object of theological reflection but that people were equipped by the churches, through discipleship, including theological education, for life in the political arena. The dilemma is that those formed by the churches often follow different political creeds.

Margaret Thatcher, so Young reports, was both formed by Methodism and had an ongoing interest in theology – as a leisure activity (!) – whilst simultaneously being severely criticized by many in the churches for her lack of Christian morality.[57] Further, issues such as compromise, pragmatism or expediency are rarely the subject of theological reflection, the overriding concern is with traditional theological discussions.

Judging from what Habgood goes on to discuss, it is unlikely that he meant to refer to Hauerwas or other anti-liberal theologies. Habgood's Christian beliefs translate into three controlling pointers for Christian involvement in political life; these relate to the daily business of political life, in part by limiting the extent to which truth can be known by the churches. They are: there can be legitimate difference between Christians and this limits the possibility of 'moral absolutism' in political comment; a concern with the quality of political debate as opposed to presenting moral certainties or truth; and a recognition that certain, rare, issues, such as anti-racism will unite all Christians.

It is John Habgood who speaks, at least about compromise, when all around him are silent; he wrote, as an appendix at the end of *Church and Nation in a Secular Age*, a short essay entitled 'Theological Reflections on Compromise'.[58] Habgood attempts to be more positive about compromise than is usual amongst theologians by seeking to set limits to a 'middle ground' which is neither compromise for compromise's sake nor the relentless adhesion to moral principle. What is removed is theological absoluteness, the mystery of God providing space for error, incomplete knowledge and surprising revelations of the divine. Compromise is thereby permissible, appropriate, and no longer the opposite of theology. In one sense this is encouraging for those who are, or have been, compromised, but the questions remain of when and how often compromise is permitted, that is, what are the boundaries and limits of political compromise?

Analysing the Theological in Political Life

In his book *Deity and Domination* David Nichols draws an important distinction between ethical reflection and an analysis of the theological in politics.[59] There are more ways for religion and politics to relate than through ethics alone, although ethics can have a place. 'Subtle connections are made and conclusions drawn as a result of the analogy – sometimes explicit, frequently implicit – between God and the state.'[60] The following is the legitimization of Nichols's study: 'The primary concern of this volume is, however, to discover "what is going on" – to borrow a phrase from Richard Niebuhr – rather than to determine what we ought to do or think about God and the state.'[61] This is not a general analysis, in the sense of defining underlying philosophies, principles or values, but a specific analysis of theological motifs, themes, metaphors and images, an acknowledgement of the ongoing relevance of the Christian legacy in Western society.[62] Nichols does not analyse so that he can criticize the decisions of politicians either directly, by identifying and condemning the values or principles which underpin their decisions, or indirectly by proposing alternative visions of the social order. Nichols remains a theologian when confronted by political activity, its life and business.

Reformist political theologians function like politicians, or civil servants or lobbyists, by engaging critically with the values or principles implicit or explicit in political decisions. But, and this is where we can envisage something queer, reformist political theologians are neither politicians nor civil servants; in other words reformist political theologians adopt the guise of that which they are not, they imitate but do not commit or belong. They want to speak to politicians, but from afar, have intimacy and influence whilst being above the fray, to belong to the court whilst living in the country. Reformist political theology is bound by its self-imposed exile, it is restricted to a twilight role of neither politician nor social, economic or political theorist. It pretends to be a politician, or to have the ear of politicians, by promoting a concern for values, visions, principles and philosophies but, at the same moment, it neglects compromise, expediency, opportunism, friendships, alliance building, desire and ambition, the very stuff of politics and politicians. Reformist political theology is not what it purports to be, it is an illusion; ultimately it is politics without politicians, something queer indeed.

There are two points, in different ways problematic, on which to finish, two responses to that which seems queer in reformist political theology. The first is to follow the urgings of the Roman Catholic Bishops of England and Wales and recommend a political career as a proper vocation. This is ultimately the outcome of Habgood's position although he is keen to ensure political programmes are not divinized, the sin against the Spirit in reformist political theology. The second is to follow Nichols's lead and suggest political theology should engage in analysis of the theological in politics rather than offering prescriptions, guidance and direction. This is not the same as identifying or advocating certain values, underlying philosophies or visions; the theological is much more specific than the good, the ethical. An analysis of the theological depends on a belief that the Christian legacy still has meaning in contemporary politics. It is an affirmation that the secular/sacred divide has limited value in our understanding of contemporary political life. In a sense it is to take the work and life of politicians and treat these as what they are, namely theological texts, and thereby explain politicians to themselves. In other words what we could say in conclusion is that political theology might be either political or theological, but it should beware of seeking to be both together, and ending up as neither.

Notes

1. W. Temple, *Christianity and Social Order*, 1976 edition (London: Shepheard-Walwyn, 1942).
2. Ibid., p. 58.
3. Ibid.
4. P. Hinchliff, *Holiness and Politics* (London: Darton, Longman & Todd, 1982).
5. Ibid., p. 35.
6. Ibid., p. 19.
7. It is recognized that the term 'political theology' may for some mean a Marxist informed theology associated with the 1960s particularly in Germany. This is not the sense meant here where it refers to the efforts of theologians to engage with the generality of political life and activity. The descriptor 'reformist' is intended to limit the scope of this chapter, since there is not room to examine properly the radical orthodoxy of Milbank, nor the virtue theological ethics of Hauerwas, nor theologies of liberation. This said, some of what is argued in the chapter is clearly applicable to these various schools. The reformist tradition has been chosen for analysis because it remains the predominant political theology within the churches, especially their hierarchies.
8. D. Forrester, *Beliefs, Values and Politics. Conviction Politics in a Secular Age* (Oxford: Clarendon Press, 1989), p. 20.
9. D. Forrester, *Christian Justice and Public Policy* (Cambridge: Cambridge University Press, 1997).
10. H. Clark, *The Church Under Thatcher* (London: SPCK, 1993), p. 32.
11. J. M. Gustafson, 'An Analysis of Church and Society Social Ethical Writings', *The Ecumenical Review*, 40/2 (1988), pp. 267–78.
12. Ibid., p. 272.
13. Ibid., p. 276.
14. Ibid.
15. T. Blair, *Faith in Politics*, address to Christian Socialist Movement conference, 29th March 2001. The text is available on the Labour

Party website and also in a CSM pamphlet entitled *Faith in Politics* (London: CSM, 2001), pp. 9–14.

16. Ibid., pp. 9–10. It should be noted that the multi-faith element of Blair's creed pre-dated September 11th. Some, for example Don Cupitt 'The New Labour Project: Modernization and Personalism', *Political Theology*, 1 (1999), pp. 19–26 and Mark Chapman, 'Pluralism, Welfare and the 'Common Good': Three Varieties of Christian Socialism', *Political Theology*, 2 (2000), pp. 33–56, have argued that what I have described as Blair's liberalism is a form of personalism based on the work of John Macmurray. This seems possible, and of course Blair's creed will develop, without altering the basic point.

17. *Faith in Politics*, p. 10.

18. Ibid., p. 9.

19. H. Young, *One of Us. A Biography of Margaret Thatcher*, final edition (London: Pan Books, 1993), p. 100. Thatcher was Secretary of State for Education in the Heath government.

20. Ibid., pp. 104–5.

21. Ibid., p. 104.

22. Ibid.

23. Young states that Thatcher's 'good fortune' was 'to be propelled into the leadership when the party was ready for a return to fundamentalist Conservatism of a kind she was most at ease with'. Ibid., p. 101.

24. A. Clark, *Diaries* (London: Weidenfeld and Nicolson, 1993). Clark was a military historian.

25. D. Macintyre, *Mandelson and the Making of New Labour* (London: Harper Collins, 2000), p. 509.

26. Ibid.

27. A. Rawnsley, *Servants of the People. The Inside Story of New Labour* (London: Hamish Hamilton, 2000), p. 144.

28. Ibid., p. 145.

29. J. Rentoul, *Tony Blair*, revised edition (London: Warner Books, 1996), see for example p. 356. Rawnsley makes the workings of New Labour relations the central theme in his book.

30. J. Major, *The Autobiography* (London: HarperCollins Publishers, 2000), p. 698.

31. Ibid., p. 733.

32. H. Walton, "'If this Political Party were a House…'": Theological

Reflections upon the Style and Spirit of New Labour', *Political Theology*, 1 (1999), pp. 11–18.

33. R. Crossman, (ed.), *The God that Failed* (Washington: Regnery Gateway, 1983). Crossman was a Cabinet Minister under Wilson from 1964–1970.

34. Ibid., p. 7.

35. Ibid.

36. A. Koestler, in Crossman, *God that Failed*, p. 15.

37. Ibid., p. 20.

38. Ibid., p. 34.

39. Ibid., p. 50.

40. Ibid., p. 51.

41. R. Wright, in Crossman, *God that Failed*, p. 154.

42. Ibid., p. 155.

43. Ibid., p. 156.

44. Ibid.

45. For a discussion of 'political religions' see W. Ustorf, 'Confronting Political Religion with Divine Religion: Christian Strategies of Re-evangelization in the 1930s', *Political Theology*, 3/1 (2001), pp. 22–31 and his book *Sailing on the Next Tide: Missions, Missiology, and the Third Reich* (Bern: Peter Lang, 2000).

46. H. Montefiore, *Christianity and Politics* (Basingstoke: The Macmillan Press Ltd., 1990), pp. 75–6.

47. K. Medhurst and G. Moyser, 'Lambeth Palace, The Bishops and Politics', in G. Moyser (ed.), *Church and Politics Today. The Role of the Church of England in Contemporary Politics* (Edinburgh: T. & T. Clark, 1985), p. 77 and p. 93.

48. G. Moyser, 'The Church of England and Politics: Patterns and Trends', in *Church and Politics Today*, p. 10.

49. R. Plant, 'The Anglican Church and the Secular State', in *Church and Politics Today*, p. 322.

50. J. Habgood, *Church and Nation in a Secular Age* (London: Darton, Longman & Todd, 1983), p. 61.

51. G. Ecclestone, *The Church of England and Politics: Reflections on Christian Social Engagement*, General Synod Paper GS457 (London: Church House, 1981), p. 78.

52. Catholic Bishops' Conference of England and Wales, *The Common Good and the Catholic Church's Social Teaching* (Manchester: Global

Communications Ltd., 1997), p. 15.

53. Ibid.

54. *Church and Nation*, p. 168.

55. Ibid.

56. For a discussion of this analysis of Stanley Hauerwas see N. Biggar, 'Is Stanley Hauerwas Sectarian?', in M. T. Nation & S. Wells (eds.), *Faithfulness and Fortitude. In Conversation with the Theological Ethics of Stanley Hauerwas* (Edinburgh: T. & T. Clark, 2000), pp. 141–60.

57. *One of Us*, p. 418.

58. *Church and Nation*, pp. 179–89.

59. D. Nichols, *Deity and Domination. Images of God and the State in the Nineteenth and Twentieth Centuries* (London: Routledge, 1989).

60. Ibid., p. 2.

61. Ibid., p. 1.

62. Another illustration of this theological analysis of 'what is going on' is Cupitt's critique of the 'personalism' that underpins the thinking of New Labour, see note 16.

The Mother of All The Buddhas

Peggy Morgan

Riding on the precious wheels of Compassion and Wisdom
Pulled by the horse of good heart and benevolent motivation
May you be granted the great fortune of auspicious conditions
To naturally arrive at the glorious garden of limitless freedom
(Ringu Tulku, *Invocation for The Year of the Water Horse*)

It is a great pleasure to be asked to contribute to a volume which is
commemorative and celebratory of the work and life of Philip Budd.
The theme is an apt one, since wisdom is not only a focus in Philip's
work, but also a quality of his character. To me this is important, for my
own home environment gave me a strong sense that the pursuit of
education and learning was not so much a desire for knowledge as a path
to understanding and wisdom. This wisdom was seen as a gentle, reflective
quality which made people more humane and was therefore quite different
from the aggression and cutting argumentation of those deemed to be
merely academic or clever. Philip is endowed with this wisdom quality
and I and my family owe much to his personal friendship and the generous
hospitality and kindness, which are surely the practical outpourings of
wisdom, offered over many years by Philip with Janet whilst we were
colleagues at Westminster College and since. During these years Philip
and I sometimes shared our sadness that the emphases and practices of
much contemporary education are far from wise. In this regard I have
often recalled the now famous lines of T. S. Eliot, who was much
influenced by Buddhist ideas, and it seems apt in the light of Philip's
interests to include both poetry and prayer/invocation in the first section
of this chapter.[1]

Endless invention, endless experiment,
Brings knowledge of motion but not of stillness
Knowledge of speech but not of silence;
Knowledge of words but ignorance of the Word.
All our knowledge brings us nearer to our ignorance,
All our ignorance brings us nearer to death,
But nearness to death no nearer to God.
Where is the life we have lost in living?
Where is the wisdom we have lost in knowledge?
Where is the knowledge we have lost in information?
The cycles of heaven in twenty centuries
Bring us farther from God and nearer to the Dust.[2]

I originally followed my own quest for meaning and a desire to reflect on matters of ultimate concern, which is what I saw as the framework for a quest for wisdom, by reading a degree in Christian Theology. I found at the time I did my degree little exploration of what constituted wisdom in either the biblical scholarship, early church history or contemporary thinking at which we looked. It was not until later that I read and was impressed by Peter Brown's description of Augustine of Hippo's search for wisdom and also reflected on the centrality of that concept in the dedication of the key church in Constantinople/Byzantium to Haghia or Sancta Sophia, Holy Wisdom.[3] What had dominated my earlier work on Augustine was the examination of the roots of a doctrine of original sin in his work and the dramatic events of his final conversion experience. Other doctrinal emphases in the course that I did were on justification by faith and theories of the atonement. These may, of course, be no more than features of theological education at a particular time and place. However, when I later came to study Buddhism I found a completely different language world and analysis of the human condition, with wisdom given a seminal place.

There is in Buddhist discourse an emphasis on *avijja* (Pali) *avidya* (Sanskrit), meaning spiritual ignorance or delusion, rather than sin or disobedience as the primary root of all suffering and evil in the world; and these are the characteristics which stop people seeing the true nature of things. This means that it is wisdom and understanding – *panna* (Pali) *prajna* (Sanskrit) – and not atonement and faith that are the keys to enlightenment/salvation, and that wisdom is a foundational concept which features repeatedly in contemporary as well as classical Buddhist schools of thought and practice. It was not, therefore, possible to study Buddhism without trying to discern what is meant by wisdom and how it connects with other important aspects of the Buddhist worldview, especially compassion and skilful means. Thus, despite a common focus on love and compassion, Buddhism offers a paradigm of the human condition and its resolution which has a different starting point from the Christian one and emphasizes that it is ignorance along with greed and hatred that are the qualities of an unenlightened mind and heart. This means that my first impressions in studying these two worldviews were of differences, but, as I shall point out later in this chapter, taxonomies and typologies of difference in religious traditions are rarely watertight and need in the end to be treated with caution.

What follows is a piece of thematic and descriptive phenomenology of religion. The dominant theme is obviously wisdom and by phenomenology, whatever its meaning elsewhere, I indicate an approach which seeks to present a religion as far as possible from the standpoints of those whose religion it is, that is to give empathetic insiders' perspectives, even when the researcher/scholar is herself an outsider.[4] This seems to me to be a just way of proceeding when looking at someone else's tradition. It does not have to be done thematically, since phenomenologists can also focus on one tradition 'in the round' without being comparative or even on one community in that tradition.[5] Indeed in relation to small-scale studies it has been said that anthropologists do well what phenomenologists think they do! I use the plural above of insiders'/belongers' positions, since no religion is monolithic, but contains within itself a spectrum of views and emphases. I have assumed that most of the readers of this volume will not be particularly familiar with Buddhist ideas and practices and have written accordingly, trying to keep the technical terminology to a minimum, without diacritical marks and with the use of translations for ease of approach. It will emerge as the discussion proceeds that the concept of *panna/prajna* is so interdependent with other ideas and practice that it cannot be isolated from Buddhist worldviews as a whole. This emphasis on interdependence is in itself an important part of Buddhists' own approaches.

Nyanatiloka's *Buddhist Dictionary*, which focuses on the Theravada Buddhist and therefore uses Pali terms, indicates the very wide field covered by the term *panna*, which he translates as 'understanding, knowledge, wisdom and insight'.[6] Three kinds of knowledge, he says, are the conditions for wisdom to arise. These are knowledge based on thinking for oneself, knowledge based on learning from others, and knowledge based on the mental development of concentration.

The above is our first example of the lists which fill the Buddhist scriptures, all of which overlap and interconnect. The key elements of the Buddhist path are summarized in the terms morality (*sila*), meditation (*samadhi*), and wisdom (*panna*). In this listing morality and meditation are foundational for the development of wisdom and it will not develop unless they are there. The eightfold path is an expansion of these three areas and is the more commonly quoted list, but it places the elements in a different order, wisdom being sub-divided into two qualities:

Wisdom:	right view or understanding
	right directed thoughts
Morality:	right speech
	right action
	right livelihood
Meditation:	right effort
	right mindfulness
	right concentration

Here right understanding and right thought are given as the key components of wisdom, and are listed first. These are followed by morality, unpacked as right speech, action and livelihood, and meditation seen as right effort, mindfulness and concentration. The 'right' in these steps on the path to enlightenment indicates what is appropriate for any context and is sometimes translated as 'perfect'. The emphasis of the order in the eightfold path is that some wisdom will be present for anyone to see the need to begin to tread a path to enlightenment or to make progress in the other stages; but in the end the elements are in a circular interdependence, itself a profoundly Buddhist emphasis. One is wise to realize that morality is necessary and meditation important for the spiritual path, and that living ethically and mindfully will make a person wise. Being able to think and act appropriately (rightly) is also a dimension of one's skilfulness, and it will later be seen how one of the interdependences in Buddhist ideas is that of wisdom with skilful means, which is a very important early concept that becomes a full-blown doctrine/teaching in Mahayana

Buddhism.

For the Buddhist, *citta bhavana* (Pali), the training and disciplining of the mind and heart is inseparable from, and in another list involves, body, speech and mind, the whole human being. An added dimension to this is the fact that *citta* (Pali) and *cinta* (Sanskrit) can be translated as either heart or mind and *bhavana* is sometimes suggested as the Pali term which most closely matches the concept 'religion' in English. Walpola Rahula emphasizes the interconnections: 'It is very interesting and important to note here that thoughts of selfless detachment, love and non-violence are grouped on the side of wisdom ... and that all thoughts of selfish desire, ill-will, hatred and violence are the result of a lack of wisdom – in all spheres of life whether individual, social or political.' He continues, 'Deep understanding is called 'penetration', seeing a thing in its true nature, without name and label. This penetration is possible only when the mind is free from all impurities and is fully developed through meditation.'[7]

The characteristics of a wise person are listed in the *Dhammapada* (Pali), and this text makes links with many other qualities, in particular with equanimity:

> v. 25   By endeavour, diligence, discipline and self-mastery, let the wise man make [of himself] an island that no flood can overwhelm.

> v.33   This fickle, unsteady mind, difficult to guard, difficult to control, the wise man makes straight.

> v. 81   Even as a solid rock is unshaken by the wind, so are the wise unshaken by praise or blame.

> v.82   Even as a lake, deep, extremely clear and tranquil, so do the wise become tranquil having heard the Teaching.[8]

Each verse touches another dimension of Buddhist practice linked with wisdom and also links with the many lists in which wisdom is included or its qualities unpacked.

Wisdom is one of the five Buddhist powers or spiritual faculties, also translated as 'virtues'. In English these are 'faith; vigour or energy; mindfulness; concentration and wisdom'.[9] The term translated as 'faith' in this list is more accurately rendered as 'trustful confidence' which is strongly linked to the practice of meditation, unpacked as vigour, mindfulness and concentration. Faith is always balanced by wisdom, and therefore is never 'blind'. Nyanatiloka discusses the balance needed between these elements 'for excessive faith with deficient wisdom leads to blind belief, whilst excessive wisdom with deficient faith leads to cunning. In the same way, great energy with weak concentration leads to restlessness, whilst strong concentration with deficient energy leads to indolence'.[10]

Another list in which wisdom features is that of the perfections or *paramita* (Sanskrit). These are particularly linked with the stages of the bodhisattva path in Mahayana Buddhism, to which I shall return. The lists vary. Nyanatiloka gives the list which is quoted below in Pali with translations. All of these qualities that are listed are illustrated in the *jataka* (birth) stories which describe the previous births or lives of someone on the path to enlightenment, particularly *Gotama* (Pali) *Gautama* (Sanskrit) Buddha. In the Mahayana scriptures the list is shorter and contains only the five qualities marked by an asterisk with the addition of meditation:

*dana	giving
*sila	morality
nekkhama	renunciation
*panna	wisdom
*virya	energy
*khanti	patience
sacca	truthfulness
adhitthano	resolution
metta	loving kindness
upekkha	equanimity

Peter Harvey lists the perfections in relationship to the ideal path of the Mahayana bodhisattva.[11] Here the six Mahayana perfections are extended to ten to tie in with the ten stages of the bodhisattva's progress. The terms are given in Sanskrit and are:

dana	generosity
sila	moral virtue
ksanti	patience
virya	vigour
dhyana	meditation
prajna	wisdom

upaya kausalya	skilful means
pranidhana	aspiration
bala	power
jnana	spiritual knowledge

In another type of list 'the faculty of wisdom' is described:

> that is comprehension, investigation, close investigation, investigation of mental states, discernment, discrimination, differentiation, cleverness, skill, subtlety, clear understanding, thought, examination, breath, sagacity, leading, insight, clear consciousness, as a goad, as power, as a sword, as terraced heights, as light, effulgence, splendour, as a jewel; lack of confusion … right view.[12]

This quotation indicates that *prajna* includes what Paul Williams calls 'worldly or conventional prajna ... understanding through investigation of grammar, medicine or some other mundane skill' as well as 'ultimate prajna, the understanding which results from an investigation into the way things really are'; this also includes 'a meditative absorption' which goes beyond conceptualization and duality.[13]

To be wise is to see the truth about the way things are or to penetrate to the reality of things as they are in themselves. This is a possible translation of the Buddhist term *dhamma* (Pali) *dharma* (Sanskrit), which can also be translated more prosaically as teaching or law. Realizing this truth fully is the end of suffering, the blowing out of the fires of greed, hatred and ignorance which is *Nibbana* (Pali) *Nirvana* (Sanskrit). Being contextual makes concepts such as wisdom, along with the other elements of the path, very fluid. That is why Thich Nhat Hanh, the Vietnamese Zen monk, who is one of the key figures in the development of engaged Buddhism, prefers the word 'understanding' to 'wisdom' and says:

> Understanding is like water flowing in a stream. Wisdom and knowledge are solid and can block our understanding. In Buddhism knowledge is regarded as an obstacle for understanding. If we take something to be the truth, we may cling to it so much that even if the truth comes and knocks at our door, we won't want to let it in. We have to be able to transcend our previous knowledge the way we climb up a ladder. If we are on the fifth rung and think that we are very high, there is no hope for us to step up to the sixth. We must learn to transcend our own views. Understanding, like water, can flow, can penetrate.[14]

Wisdom and Compassion

Wisdom is not only inseparable from and interconnected with morality and meditation, but also intertwined with compassion. These two, *panna* (wisdom) and *karuna* (compassion) in Pali, are two of the four 'divine or ultimate states of mind', the other two being *metta* (loving kindness) and *upekkha* (equanimity). Wisdom and compassion balance each other and can be identified with the heart/mind polarisation which the use of the word *citta/cinta* seeks to re-unite:

> Here compassion represents love, charity, kindness, tolerance and such noble qualities on the emotional side, or qualities of the heart, while wisdom would stand for the intellectual side or qualities of the mind. If one develops only the emotional, neglecting the intellectual, one may become a good-hearted fool; while to develop only the intellectual side neglecting the emotional may turn one into a hard-hearted intellect without feeling for others.[15]

Since wisdom and compassion are two aspects of the enlightened heart/mind for Buddhists any attempt to contrast the Buddhist and Christian idioms as one or the other, that is Buddhism as a wisdom path and Christianity as a path of love, is inaccurate. In making this distinction between the two different paths, Aloysius Pieris, the Sri Lankan Jesuit writer, in *Love Meets Wisdom* does say that this difference in emphasis is a language barrier to Buddhist–Christian dialogue and that 'any valid spirituality, Buddhist or Christian, as the history of each religion attests, does retain both poles of religious experience – namely the gnostic and the agapeic'.[16] Pieris uses the Greek terms for knowledge (*gnosis*) and love (*agape*) in his discussion and advocates a dialogue which rediscovers both poles in each tradition:

> For I believe that there is a Christian gnosis which is necessarily agapeic; and there is also a Buddhist agape which remains gnostic. In other words, deep within each one of us there is a Buddhist and Christian engaged in a profound encounter that each tradition – Buddhist and Christian – has registered in the doctrinal articulation of each religion's core experience. What seems impossible – the interpenetration of the two irreducibly distinct idioms – has already taken place both within Christianity and

within Buddhism.[17]

Pieris's experience of a perceived contrast between love and wisdom emerges out of his life in a Sri Lankan Theravada Buddhist context. In Mahayana Buddhism, especially in Tibetan Mahayana, there is perhaps a much more explicit emphasis on the inseparability of Wisdom and Compassion, though the roots of that union are certainly there in the Theravada Pali texts.

Pieris echoes, and in the end argues against, the desire scholars have often had to typologize religions and make a taxonomy of religions. One of the most recent examples of this is in Hans Kung and Julia Ching's *Christianity and Chinese Religions* where they identify three great river systems of religions:

The prophetic religions:	Judaism, Christianity and Islam
The mystical religions:	Jainism, Buddhism and Hinduism
The religions of wisdom:	Chinese religions[18]

There are various flaws in this taxonomy. First, why is part of it based on geography and part on religious traditions listed as though they are monolithic entities? Secondly, Judaism, Christianity and Islam all have strong streams of mysticism within them. Thirdly, the term 'Chinese religions', as a different kind of descriptive term based on geography, *includes some* forms of Buddhism in addition to Daoism and Confucianism. Fourthly, some would contest that the great classical systems originating in China, Daoism and Confucianism fit easily into the category 'religion'. Fifthly, wisdom is a strand in all forms of Buddhism in its many geographical regions and is not part of Chinese Buddhism alone.

Wisdom and Skilful Means

'Skilful means' or 'skill in means' is the second most important quality or concept interlinked with wisdom on which I wish to focus. In the popular images of the bodhisattva of infinite compassion in the Mahayana Buddhist traditions (Chenrezig in Tibetan), Avalokiteshvara is pictured with a thousand arms.[19] In each of the thousand hands of the 'Lord who looks down' (the literal translation of his name) on the sufferings of the

world, there is a manifestation of compassion, something that will help
suffering beings such as a bowl of medicine or a pot of water. On the
palm of each hand there is an eye. With these thousand eyes
Avalokiteshvara can discern all the needs of a suffering world. For him to
be of any help at all the problems need to be *seen* aright. To echo the
words of Walpola Rahula quoted above, the good-hearted fool with a
water pot will be of little use without the skill to make appropriate use of
it and the person of hard-hearted intellect who sees the issues will be of
little help without a water pot to administer care. I always see the
complementarity of compassion, wisdom and skilful means as not unlike
the balance of qualities needed to be a good social worker. If there is too
much compassion and empathy then identification can be so close that it
is difficult to stand back and make decisions. On the other hand if there is

only incisive, cutting discernment, action can be efficient but deeply unsupportive.

Skilful means is especially illustrated in the many stories of *The Lotus Sutra* where, for example, a wise and compassionate father chooses to disguise himself and travels far to seek out his erring and debased son and gradually and anonymously give him back his full dignity and place in society.[20] According to one delightful Buddhist folk text *The Buddha's Lore Among the Birds*, Avalokiteshvara, by his skilful means, is able to give his teachings 'in any tongue that a being may grasp them' and transforms himself into a cuckoo in order to teach the birds.[21]

The Mother of the Buddhas

Mahayana Buddhist literature has a special collection of texts, some of which I have already mentioned. These are called collectively the *Prajnaparamita Sutras*, the *Perfection of Wisdom* texts. Some of these are very long and composite (100,000 verses) and some are condensed distillations of the teaching (for example the *Diamond* and the *Heart Sutras*). Edward Conze has been one of the foremost interpreters of these and preferred the translation 'the wisdom that has gone beyond' or 'transcendental wisdom' for 'the perfection of wisdom'. He thought that perfection was a rather moralistic term in English and that the term *paramita* has more to do with that which has gone beyond all the guidelines of knowledge and morality that are part of worldly systems. Wisdom is also something that cannot be grasped in any way, for this would imply limitation. The wisdom that has gone beyond is dismantled by the vision and dream quality of the descriptions in the texts. These descriptions open up a way of thinking and living that is flexible and flowing (see the quotation from Thich Nhat Hanh given above). But to this sense of flexibility is also added the image of the *vajra*, the thunderbolt or diamond quality of wisdom which cuts through ignorance. In this image wisdom is perceptive, incisive, indestructible and cutting. The bodhisattva Manjushri, who personifies the perfection of wisdom, likewise shows the interdependence of the attributes under discussion. In a typical portrayal, he is shown as a young man carrying in his upraised right hand a two-edged or double-edged sword ready and able to cut through illusion.[22] In his left hand is a lotus, which is also carried by Avalokiteshvara and is a symbol of enlightenment and the pure beauty of compassion in Buddhism. In this lotus rests a text of the *Prajnaparamita Sutra*. But in another, perhaps surprising, dimension

of the iconography, the *vajra* (the cutting diamond/thunderbolt) symbolizes compassion and the bell wisdom, a seeming reversal of symbolism. They can be held separately in different hands or combined into a *vajra*-bell

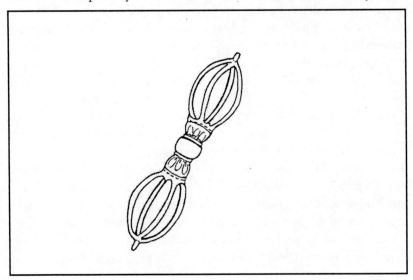

sceptre.[23]

Prajnaparamita texts usually begin with an invocation to the perfection of wisdom which is their focus. A typical invocation is 'Homage to the Perfection of Wisdom, the Lovely, the Holy'. Edward Conze points out that the term here translated 'Lovely' can also be translated as 'Lady' and the term translated 'Holy' can also mean 'Noble' and that the perfection of wisdom can be personified as female and as the 'Mother of the Buddhas and Bodhisattvas'.[24] In *The Perfection of Wisdom in Eight Thousand Lines* Conze translates the hymn to the perfection of wisdom:

> The perfection of wisdom gives light … she is worthy of homage.
> She is unstained, the entire world cannot stain her.
> She is a source of light, and from everyone in the triple world she removes darkness, and she leads away from the blinding darkness caused by the defilements and bywrong views.
> In her we can find shelter. Most excellent are her works.
> She makes us seek the safety of the wings of enlightenment.
> She brings light to the blind, she brings light so that all fear and stress may be forsaken …
> She guides to the path those who have strayed on to a bad road …
> She is the mother of the bodhisattvas …
> She cannot be crushed. She protects the unprotected.[25]

Texts such as the *Heart Sutra* continue after their invocation to focus on the bodhisattva Avalokiteshvara, 'the Lord who looks down' (on the sufferings of the world), who is the personification of compassion and who, in the complementarity of wisdom and compassion that we have discussed above, can be seen as the consort of the female perfection of wisdom. But in far eastern Buddhism Avalokiteshvara becomes conflated with the Chinese 'goddess of mercy' and becomes the bodhisattva Quan-yin or Kuan-yin. In Japan, Kannon as she is known, is a very popular figure and images of her are made both in delicate white porcelain to stand on home shelves and also over fifty metres high to dominate the landscape.[26]

Needless to say those writing about the place of women in Buddhism such as Diana Paul and Rita Gross have found the female and matriarchal images here rich ones and both point out that Kuan-yin and Prajnaparamita are the two feminine personifications in Mahayana Buddhism.[27] But they also point out that in the text of the popular *Lotus Sutra*, Kuan-yin, out of

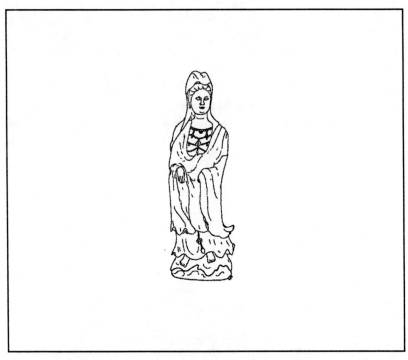

compassion and using her skilful means, assumes thirty-three forms in all, of which seven are female, and that in the end it is the one who perceives through enlightenment who has the *dharma* (truth, teaching), which is neither male nor female.

In Vajrayana Buddhism the feminine aspect of enlightenment is also portrayed when the perfection of wisdom is shown as the 'desired lover'. 'In his constant contemplation of wisdom [the male student] is like a man in love who constantly thinks of his beloved, especially when separated from her.'[28] In the art of Vajrayana Buddhism, the mystical union of compassion and wisdom are illustrated by the father-mother pairs:

> Quite deliberately *Wisdom and Compassion: The Sacred Art of Tibet* begins with this startling image that shows the Buddha – the same Buddha most often presented as a fatherly monk – in father-mother union form, in an aspect that is electrifyingly physical. The father-mother union image of the Buddha as Supreme Bliss ... is not an example of erotic art ... The father-mother union is a manifestation of the Buddha's highest spiritual essence, of enlightenment as the union of wisdom and compassion ...

the female (mother) represents transcendent wisdom ... the male (father) ... represents compassion for all beings, which is the natural expression of such wisdom.[29]

The mother who is transcendent wisdom also stands alone in her role as the mother of all the Buddhas and Bodhisattvas.

The Buddhas in the world systems in the ten directions
Bring to mind this perfection of wisdom as their mother.
The saviours of the world who were in the past, and also are now in the ten directions,
Have issued from her, and so will the future ones be.
She is the one who shows this world (for what it is), she is the genetrix, the mother of the Buddhas.[30]

In this exploration I have sought to show that, starting with a concept as richly significant as wisdom, we are immediately networked, as illustrated in the image of the jewel net of India, into a whole worldview that is Buddhist. Concepts mirror and complement each other, are expressed in metaphor and iconography as much as philosophy, and are inextricably linked to practice. Wisdom is both the foundation and fruit of a path that is also characterized by morality and meditation. The partners of the sword and bell of wisdom are the lotus and diamond of compassion. Wisdom enables truth to be taught skilfully and action to be taken in the variety of contexts in which sentient beings suffer. It finds expression in ways that challenge all stereotypes of religion entombed in masculine hierarchies. Philip has shown his sound instinct and insight in making such a theme, though in another textual tradition, a focus of research. I hope that the above chapter by extending the canon will provide further stimulus for his and others' work.

Notes

1. See C. McNelly Kearns, *T. S. Eliot and Indic Traditions: A Study in Poetry and Belief* (Cambridge: Cambridge University Press, 1987).
2. T. S. Eliot, 'Choruses from The Rock', *Selected Poems* (London: Faber and Faber, 1954), p. 97.
3. P. Brown, *Augustine of Hippo* (Berkeley: University of California Press, 1969).
4. For an examination of the diverse meanings of the term see: J. Cox, *Expressing The Sacred: An Introduction to The Phenomenology of Religion* (Harare: University of Zimbabwe Publication, 1992); G. Flood, *Beyond Phenomenology* (London: Cassell, 1999); W. B. Kristenson, *The Meaning of Religion*, Eng. trans. (The Hague: Mouton, 1960); E. Sharpe, *Comparative Religion: A History*, 2nd edn. (London: Duckworth, 1986), chapter 10; N. Smart, *The Phenomenon of Religion* (New York: Herder and Herder, 1973); G. Van der Leeuw, *Religion in Essence and Manifestation* (New York: Harper and Row, 1963).
5. N. Smart, *The Phenomenon of Christianity* (London: William Collins and Sons Ltd., 1979).
6. Nyanatiloka, *Buddhist Dictionary*, 4th edn. (Kandy: Buddhist Publication Society, 1980), p. 150.
7. W. Rahula, *What the Buddha Taught* (London: Gordon Fraser, 1978), p. 49.
8. Ibid., pp. 126–7.
9. See Nyanatiloka, *Buddhist Dictionary*, p. 35 and pp. 78–9 and *Buddhist Scriptures*, trans. Edward Conze (Middlesex: Penguin, 1959), pp. 181–9.
10. Nyanatiloka, *Buddhist Dictionary*, p. 35 and pp. 78–9.
11. P. Harvey, *An Introduction to Buddhism* (Cambridge: Cambridge University Press, 1990), pp. 122–4.
12. *Buddhist Texts Through the Ages*, trans. Edward Conze (Oxford: Bruno Cassirer, n/d), p. 65.
13. P. Williams, *Mahayana Buddhism* (London: Routledge, 1989), pp. 42–

5.

14. Thich Nhat Hanh, *The Heart of Understanding* (Berkeley: Parallax Press, 1988), p. 8.

15. Rahula, *What the Buddha Taught*, p. 46.

16. A. Pieris, *Love Meets Wisdom: A Christian Experience of Buddhism* (Maryknoll: Orbis, 1988), p. 111.

17. Ibid., p. 113.

18. H. Kung and J. Ching, *Christianity and Chinese Religions* (New York: Doubleday, 1989), pp. ix–xix.

19. The three illustrations that follow are all by Catharine Morgan from the private publication by Peggy Morgan and Catharine Morgan, *Buddhist Iconography*, n/d. This is available from the author.

20. *Scripture of the Lotus Blossom of the Fine Dharma (The Lotus Sutra)*, trans. Leon Hurvitz (New York: Columbia University Press, 1976), chapter 4.

21. *The Buddha's Lore Among the Birds*, trans. Edward Conze (Oxford: Bruno Cassirer, 1974), *passim*.

22. M. M. Rhie and R. A. F. Thurman, *Wisdom and Compassion: The Sacred Art of Tibet* (London: The Royal Academy of Arts, 1991), p. 371.

23. Ibid. *passim*.

24. *Buddhist Wisdom Books*, trans. Edward Conze, 2nd edn. (London: George Allen and Unwin, 1975), p. 77.

25. *The Perfection of Wisdom in Eight Thousand Lines*, trans. Edward Conze (California: Four Seasons, 1973), p. 135.

26. H. Bechert and R. Gombrich, *The World of Buddhism* (London: Thames and Hudson, 1984), p. 179.

27. D. Y. Paul, *Women in Buddhism* (Berkeley: Asian Humanities Press, 1979) and R. M. Gross, *Buddhism After Patriarchy* (New York: SUNY, 1993).

28. Gross, *Buddhism After Patriarchy*, pp. 75–7.

29. Rhie and Thurman, *Wisdom and Compassion*, p. 17.

30. *The Perfection of Wisdom in Eight Thousand Lines*, quoted by Gross, *Buddhism After Patriarchy*, p. 76.

Body, Mind and Spirit: Westminster College's Contribution to Higher Education

Tim Macquiban

Introduction

For the past twenty years Philip Budd has been associated with Westminster College, contributing to the development of what became one of the largest providers of full-time, part-time and distance learning courses in theology and religious studies. He has shaped the understanding of two generations of those engaged in biblical and hermeneutical studies at Westminster. In this, he stands at the end of a long tradition stretching back 150 years in which the Methodist Church, through the College, has helped form teachers, ministers and preachers, and those serving the community in many different ways in what John Wesley would have called 'scriptural holiness'. Though not himself a Methodist, he has had a warm sympathy for the aims of Methodism, engaging in a dialogue with society and exploring theology in its social context, out of a regard for a holiness which was not purely personal but social in its application.

As we celebrate 150 years of Methodism's contribution to higher education through Westminster, it is a suitable moment to reflect on what the College, founded in 1851, has offered in the way of a distinctive ethos and activity on behalf of the Methodist Church, its sponsoring body. Westminster is one of four Church institutions involved in higher education (more broadly than theological education) in what the latest Church report, *The Essence of Education*, sets out as its primary objectives. Education is about the whole person, of whatever age or ability, in body, mind and spirit. It is about allowing all to reach their full God-given potential in their doing and being.[1] The spiritual and moral dimensions of education, upheld by the 1944 Education Act, along with the mental and physical development of individuals, are important considerations for all Methodists (and other Christians) involved in schools, colleges and universities. As Rupert Davies's question posed, 'Is a child [and student] in school being prepared for life on this earth only, or for eternal life?'[2] But the context of the College's contribution to society is very different from that of the founder of Methodism and his views on education in the eighteenth century.

The Wesleyan Legacy

John Wesley had a methodical approach to all things, including education. His life was ruled by his need for busyness. It was modelled on his Oxford days when every moment of his day was scrutinized for usefulness in his quest for holy living. This method of pursuing Christian discipleship meant that the timetabled approach which disciplined the individual believer was his abiding legacy to educationalists.[3] His diary entries reveal the busyness which he recorded in detail. One example from the Georgia missionary days illustrates his approach:

TUESDAY, May 4 (1736)
4am   Private Prayer
5   Read Prayers, expounded (25 there)
6   German
6.15   Breakfast
6.45   With Germans
11   Trustees' Garden; Ecclesiastical History, Hebrew Psalm
12   Fleury's History
12.30 Dinner
1   German
1.45   Slept
2   German
3.30   Miss Musgrove and Miss Fawcet, mostly religious talk
4   Garden, with Miss Fawcet, religious talk
4.30   Tea, religious talk (necessary)
5   Religious talk with Miss Fawcet (she seemed affected)
5.45   Mostly religious talk
6.30   Supper

7	Read Greek New Testament with them
7.45	Prayers
8	Expounded
8.20	With Germans, sang
9.30	Prayed

He even graded himself as to his state of grace for each time of the day. And he recorded times of mercy when he was spared impure thoughts. That day he had them in the hour he was studying German![4]

His reading centred on the Bible but was not exclusively restricted to it. Wesley was a child of the Enlightenment but also the inheritor of Renaissance humanism, able to discover the truth for himself within the givenness of the divine revelation in Scripture.[5] The breadth of Wesley's reading was translated into the curricular studies he encouraged in his followers. Books were generally seen as a 'means of awakening' people and leading them to salvation.[6] He created a *Christian Library* of over fifty volumes to broaden their reading. He gathered the people together in small groups for their mutual support, discipline and exposition of Scripture. He encouraged the development of Sunday Schools in his later years as a means of reaching a wider number of children, especially of the poor, aware that for many 'family religion is shamefully wanting'.[7] This emphasis on the young became the predominant evangelistic thrust of the early nineteenth century: 'Let our people's children be regularly instructed in the principles of religion, and subjected to proper discipline, from six to seventeen years of age, and they will acquire a considerable share of religious knowledge.'[8]

As the National schools pitched Anglicans into the provision of elementary education and British schools rivalled the Establishment with their own unsectarian (but Christian) teaching, Methodism at first was content to concentrate its resources on the Bible-based Sunday Schools, leaving the day school provision to others. But its fear of aggressive Anglicanism and resurgent Catholicism led it reluctantly to enter into the arena of voluntary yet aided schools. Jabez Bunting, its most charismatic post-Wesleyan leader, urged them in the 1840s with a characteristic clarion call: 'Let us establish day schools ... Let us go body, mind and spirit into it.'[9]

In the United States too there was enthusiasm for Methodist involvement in elementary education. The General Conference of 1828 adopted the report of its Education Committee encouraging the growth of classical schools for 'literature, morality, industry and a practical knowledge of the arts'; but preachers like a Mr Reece fiercely resisted this development, calling students 'the greatest drones in the Gospel ministry, idlers in the vineyard, useless cucumbers of the ground who ever afflicted and cursed the Church'. And again:

> What I insist upon my brethren and sisters is this: larnin isn't religion, and eddication don't give a man the power of the spirit. It is grace and gifts that furnish the real live coals from off the altar. St. Peter was a fisherman – do you think he ever went to Yale College? ... No, no! When the Lord wanted to blow down the walls of Jericho, he didn't take a brass trumpet, or a polished French Horn; no such things; he took a ram's horn – a plain natural ram's horn – just as it grew ... He don't take one of your smooth, polite, college, larnt gentlemen, but a plain natural ram's horn sort of man like me.[10]

In Britain too there was similar resistance to higher education and learning in the 1830s. James Wood of Bristol wrote of the 'strong tendency ... generally found in the association of young men ... to corrupt one another; ... students upon leaving who think too highly of themselves, and assume a pompous air as Collegians with a display of fine words rather than the simple gospel'.[11] Presumably young women were thought not to exhibit the same tendency! Fortunately Wilbur Fisk, a College President in the States, and John Hannah in Britain pioneered the development of colleges which provided liberal arts programmes combining religion and literature, history and languages, social and human sciences in a broad sweep of education, for women as well as for men. Nevertheless anxieties continued to exist about the separation of education from the religious sphere. J. H. Rigg, Principal of Westminster College and a leading educationalist of his day, warned that 'all learning is of little value, even Biblical learning, without spiritual insight and experimental knowledge as the Divine things'.[12] Truth and goodness and beauty were to be sought in the educational process. As J. H. Newman reminded people in his *Idea of a University*, there was a need for a Christian vision to give unity and purpose to higher education.

Methodism was one of the leaders of the evangelical assault on godlessness, especially amongst the poor. Education was seen as one of its most effective agencies for moral reformation and spiritual revival.

William Vevers, in a pamphlet setting out Methodist claims to be a denomination of national importance, wrote this of the Church: 'It fosters, not destroys, a spirit of manly independence. It suppresses vice; it encourages virtue. Happy will it be for our country, when all classes, but especially the poorer classes of society, are more deeply imbued with this spirit.'[13] So when in 1851 Westminster Training College was opened to train teachers for Wesleyan day schools, its location and rationale were clearly stated by its establishing committee. It was, 'the theatre on which Protestantism and Popery shall contend for the possession of the neglected poor ... in the very midst of that dense and destitute population'.[14]

Westminster College, London

Matthew Arnold, in his work as a Government Inspector of the growing number of schools in mid-Victorian Britain, was warm in his appreciation of the contribution of the new College, in an area of London where it served a real need amongst the poor, providing a quality schooling more superior than the Board schools. Yet, despite the 'tenor of these lessons' and 'the very arrangement and organisation of the practising schools', he detected that these were of secondary importance to the maintenance of a community spirit amongst staff and students which was at the core of its commitment to a *religious* rather than a *secular* education.[15] At the heart of what Westminster was about were two principles which seemed to dominate most of the justifications for its work. One was that the knowledge and application of Scripture should be understood and communicated by all who left Westminster to teach. So worship, prayer and Bible study were integral to the life of teh community. The second was that the vocation of teachers was to engage in work amongst the poor or unchurched so that they might come not only to behave as Christian citizens but also believe. Through education there was the chance of the wider 'reformation of manners' in society which Wilberforce and other evangelicals had pressed for a generation earlier. As John Scott, the College's first Principal reported, 'If through the child he [sic] can reach the parents who may be living ungodly lives and can bring them under Christian instruction, he widens his range of usefulness.'[16] This targeting of poor areas for particular concern meant that the local practising schools helped the College to ensure that its training never became exclusively theoretical but was always rooted in an approach to and empathy for the poor.[17]

The first eighty years of the College's existence were dominated by the leadership of three Wesleyan ministers who acted not only as Principals but also as Secretaries of the Wesleyan Education Committee, determining policy for the Methodist Connexion in respect of its schools and colleges. They were John Scott (1851–68), J. H. Rigg (1868–1902) and Herbert Workman (1902–30), exercising an influence well beyond the bounds of the College at Westminster in national church and educational circles.

Scott's philosophy is most readily accessible in his published *Addresses to the Students in the Wesleyan Training Institution Westminster* (1869) which form the backbone of what he regarded as its *raison d'être*. He saw his role as training teachers who would serve in day schools which would give 'sound, intellectual, moral and religious education' enabling their pupils to enter the world of work and public service, improving their position in society.[18] While he saw a liberal approach to discipline as the way to maintain a happy and peaceful atmosphere, he was adamant that his task was to form his students in the 'habits of right feeling and of good conduct as well as of correct thinking'.[19] Teaching was a vocation and not just a job. So the chapel and the Bible study class were as important as the classroom teaching. As the preface to the *Addresses* pointed out, 'he was firmly persuaded that, to be effective, education must be based upon and strengthened by sound religious teaching'.[20]

The attention given to human development was a marked feature. The 'what it means to be human' dimension of modern Methodist approaches to education can be found in his address for 1854 in which he sets out why it is that psychology, physiology and philosophy are important aspects of the College's work. He argues for a broad curriculum which includes technology, drawing/art and singing, in order to feed and develop a questioning mind, a healthy body and a spirit nurtured by the appreciation of the place of man [sic] in God's world. Education was not to be a weary work of committing books to memory but a journey of discovery and 'an exercise unto godliness' as students were formed and transformed into the image of Christ.[21] Nevertheless, he warned of the need to guard against the temptation to neglect study of the Bible for books of geography and history and literature. For the College was 'not merely a college for learning, but also a school for manners and a nursery for religion'.[22] Secular and scriptural knowledge were to be acquired in equal measure.[23] The moral and spiritual aspects of its environment and curriculum were all-important. The questions 'What is virtue? What action is right?' were to inform all teaching. 'In hoping for moral results from education, it is not the teacher who educates religiously, but he who educates without religion, that makes himself ridiculous.'[24] For that reason Scott saw the College's work not as narrowly involved in proselytism but contributing to the moral benefit of society generally. Only incidentally was the teacher a 'valuable servant of the Church' in leading children to Christ and making Methodist members.[25]

At a later date the College adopted the motto *Virtute et Fide*. Scott put much emphasis on the College as a community in which character was formed. The social dimension of its life was important. Students were valued as self-governing members of a mutually supportive community. They were to be virtuous, seeking truth, honour, integrity and purity. They were to be religious, seeking the knowledge, fear and love of God with faith in Jesus Christ. Striving for holiness meant progress not only in academic studies but also in the development of character: 'Education, as it acquires completeness, cultivates all man's capabilities of whatever kind, and bids him never stop in the way of improvement.'[26]

The habits of perseverance, diligence, hard work, responding to the call of duty within an ordered and disciplined approach to life, were commended to all in the College.[27] The effect of the character of teachers, 'men and women of intellectual, moral and religious conformation', trained in this way was to be transformative in the classroom, exposing the evils of an unreformed life, offering a better way to the children of the poor which would improve family relations and inculcate the very nonconformist Victorian values and virtues of hard work and sobriety. In such a way the innate depravity of the lower classes 'inflamed by intoxicating drinks and sensualised minds' would be under attack from this Methodist assault on godlessness through education.[28] This preferential priority for the poor, however it can be viewed as a middle class adoption of education as an agency of social control, was a key to the understanding of Methodist motivation. Resources were to be channelled into areas of greatest social need for people who needed them most, a very Wesleyan approach from its Arminian theology.

Scott's philosophy set the tone of the College's approach for its first hundred years. J. H. Rigg developed it with a far more aggressive use of political power within the Connexion and in society to ensure that such overtly religious values were promoted and expanded within the broadening of popular education. From the start of his principalship in 1868, he sought to involve Wesleyan Methodism in a partnership with Government to provide church schools and colleges of high quality. 'If it is to be a true and vital Church … the Methodist work of education must be a work of today and tomorrow, as well as of yesterday, if it is to be founded on true and permanent principles.'[29] For Rigg, this meant the retention of church education within a developing State system with its emphasis on Bible-based (but not narrowly denominational) teaching which would inculcate Christian doctrine, principles and ethos 'to enlighten their conscience and inlay their character with the truth of our holy religion'.[30] For him also it meant that all teachers should be Christians whose own character-formation in turn moulded their pupils. The understanding of how people felt and learnt was important, hence the emphasis not on rote learning but on 'understanding' in order to develop the child's world of 'thought, imagination, sympathy', to which the insights of psychology spoke. Teachers were to be 'true-hearted … sincere and settled Christians, neither bigoted nor wavering, neither sectarian nor half-hearted'.[31]

Rigg's defence of church schools found vigorous opposition from many within Methodism, notably led by Hugh Price Hughes through his radical views expressed in *The Methodist Times*. He thought that such schools were costly and divisive and that teachers would be better employed in Christianizing the State schools. Rigg feared the rationale for church colleges would disappear if Methodist schools were to be given up. If students were allowed to withdraw from compulsory worship and Religious Education lectures then it 'would destroy all unity of Christian family life … [and] would interfere fatally with the framework of ordinary domestic and moral discipline'.[32] For he maintained that 'the bond of this institution is … the bond of fellowship'. Destroy that and the distinctiveness of a church college was destroyed.[33]

Matters came to a head around the Education Bill of 1902 which occasioned a bitter struggle between churches and with government over the extent of church control of schools and colleges and their relationship with the State. It was a watershed for Methodism and education as the Church recognized its inability to compete with others and its need to rely on State provision for the delivery of its aspirations. Rigg retired as Principal at the end of 1902, aged 81, and an era passed.[34] Methodism's legacy was to wrestle with its confessional base within an increasingly secularized State system whose avowedly Christian base still allowed Methodists to operate within the nineteenth-century framework of spiritual and moral values.

Workman, the third Wesleyan Methodist minister to preside over the College's fortunes, was able to take it forward within the wider context of developments in higher education. He recognized the tension between being a training college producing Methodist teachers for Methodist schools and aspiring to be a university college providing a range of courses for Methodists within the growing sector of higher education. As the government encouraged teaching as a graduate career, and as the upwardly mobile Methodist constituency desired to send its daughters and sons to university, so pressure on the College to adapt grew. Workman's principalship over nearly thirty years turned the College around and repositioned it. The physical environment of the College was improved with building work which included a new school, library and chapel, signifying the centrality of worship, equipping the staff and students for service in the community. The academic location of studies shifted from the provision of all studies within the institution to it being recognized as a college affiliated to the University of London, with a four year degree course by 1930 and a consequent raising of standards.[35] There remained a tension, created by the changing higher educational environment, between the desire to be recognized as a university college or the acceptance of the smallness of the College and limitation of its restricted site in Horseferry Road leading to a need to merge with other church colleges elsewhere. In this respect, Southlands College founded in 1872 for women students followed the latter path into the University of Surrey Roehampton while a relocated Westminster College positioned itself within a secular university (Oxford Brookes) in 2000.

Workman's own contribution was to give academic respectability to the institution through his distinguished teaching and writing in the area of Church History and Methodism and his recruitment of an able body of teachers equally noted in their own disciplines. Yet at the heart of the College's life was still maintained the sense of community. The classes for local preachers, the weekly College services, the Christian Union and other small group meetings, the range of activities in sports and physical education, handicrafts and music, all contributed to the ethos nurtured by successive principals in the first half of the twentieth century. Alexander Harrison, who succeeded Workman as Principal in 1930, described it thus: 'My chief concern was that the College should become a family of kindness based on simple and sincere religious convictions.'[36] This was a tradition maintained by his immediate successors, the much-loved Jock Ross (1940–53) and Trevor Hughes (1953–69).

Westminster in the Last Sixty Years : from London to Oxford

The Second World War saw the abandonment of plans to redevelop the College at its Elmstead Woods site in Kent and the evacuation of the community to Bristol for the duration of the Blitz. In 1944 the College was reoccupied with the scars of war still visible. The Chapel and the Reading Room had been destroyed in one night in June 1944 with the incalculable loss of portraits and records stored there. The restoration of College buildings was matched by the reconstruction of community life in the mould of its religious foundation. The Library was reopened in memory of Workman who died in 1951; the Chapel was remodelled to include the Harrison Pulpit, in memory of former Principal Alexander Harrison, and a new organ in memory of the war dead. Jock Ross had a difficult job restoring that which had been undone by the ravages of war. The years 1946 to 1948 were transitional. 150 men came back to do a two year certificate course rather than the four year degree course to which many aspired. There was the age difference between the two cohorts: those who had served in the war and the young men straight from school. Despite these difficulties, the 'Westminster Spirit' was rekindled anew after this period of dislocation.

From falling below 200 students, numbers slowly recovered in the post-war period. The College became affiliated to the University of London Institute of Education, established in 1949 and was its major provider of teachers in Religious Education. By the year of the centenary of the College (1951) there were about 250 students per annum training to be teachers, of whom a large majority were still Methodists who 'attend Chapel willingly as a matter of course'.[37] It was noted by some students that attendance at the Saturday Divinity lecture was considerably enhanced by the need for them to collect their bus fares required to get students down to the University in the next week![38] Within thirty years this religious observance and study was under threat in a more secular and less Methodist environment. Under the principalship of Trevor Hughes, all the old values held. He espoused 'a free, happy, self-governing community, in which all members find scope for their energies and abilities', whether in the classroom or chapel, in sports or societies.[39] Its reputation for excellence on the field and on stage was upheld.

But it was clear that, despite a royal visitation to the College in 1951, its out-of-date premises badly damaged by the war and the limitations imposed on teaching methods through insufficient numbers of staff for the small number of students who could be accommodated on site dictated that the move from Horseferry Road could not be delayed much longer. In 1953 came the decision to move, not to Kent but to Oxford where a new 'Methodist Training College near to John Wesley's own University' could be established on a green field site to the West of the city at North Hinksey.[40] The advocacy of Professor Charles Coulson and others of the University of Oxford held high hopes for some closer relationship in the future. This was only partially and temporarily realized. The efforts of the second half of the 1950s were absorbed in raising the funds necessary from Church and State and effecting the transfer to Oxford in 1959 when the buildings were completed.

Links with Horseferry Road were perpetuated in aspects of the Chapel at the heart of the new campus, through the incorporation of windows, pews and other furniture; the building was designed to house up to 400 people, in line with the anticipated expansion of numbers in teacher training. A theatre and dining hall, as well as teaching rooms and student accommodation allowed for a doubling of numbers in less than a decade. By the mid-1960s there were over 500 students, reaching a peak in the first wave of expansion in 1967 of 660 students. Inevitably something was lost in the move from the heart of London. But more space, 'an ample, purer air', the opportunity to respond to the challenge to expand numbers, and to build on the possibilities of a connection with the University of Oxford, took the place of the former close ties with the University of London.[41] Students at the College were linked to programmes organized by the Oxford University Institute of Education which connected Westminster with other educational institutions locally. At the heart of the enterprise was still the primary aim of providing Christian teachers for schools, 'men and women fully trained, well qualified, who are committed heart and soul to the service of Christ'.[42] This mixed community, increasingly dominated by the presence of women not men, was in marked contrast to the all-male presence at Horseferry Road which had given a quasi-monastic feel to the community. To assist an enlarged staff in the process of change the appointment of a full-time Chaplain was made. Trevor Hughes judged, at the end of his principalship in 1969, that 'the College is the same in its general ethos … a large community brings losses and gains; I think we are on the credit side of the ledger'.[43] It still felt like a larger religious community dedicated to the vocation of being trained as teachers.

The 1960s and 1970s saw a community still dominated by the demands of teacher education, still centred on social, cultural and spiritual activities in support of this rounded curriculum, with students taking a large measure of responsibility for their own leisure. But the changes in education in this period were to challenge the very survival of small voluntary church-related colleges such as Westminster. While the pressure to increase opportunities for higher education and to train and recruit more teachers flowed from the Newsom (1963) and Robbins (1963) reports, bringing new possibilities, there were concurrent dangers:

> As Christians we believe that education means much more than a training in certain techniques and skills; such training must be accompanied by an all-round development of the personality, and such development is usually the outcome of personal relations with teachers and fellow students.[44]

The value of small institutions would be hard to defend against the pressures of economic efficiency and rationalization.

The principalship of Donald Crompton (1969–81) was a transitional one, covering some difficult years in terms of external relationships and funding patterns, both of which came to question the long-term viability of a free-standing Methodist College of Higher Education. Expansion ceased, bringing a greater measure of stability but also limiting the number of students to be trained at the College. Fewer men came to Westminster. But the pattern of social and cultural activities continued 'as though nothing had happened'.[45] The 1971 Report to the Methodist Conference recognized that bigger changes lay ahead. The James Report (1971), recommending that all entrants to the teaching profession should in future be graduates, did not make it any easier for the College to 'survive as an independent third force'.[46] In conjunction with other voluntary sector colleges, the arguments were put to successive governments about he added-value of small church-related colleges in the higher education sector. A four year B.Ed. degree in Education with English, French, Geography,

History, Mathematics, Science and Theology/R.E. needed to be offered but initial attempts to have this validated by the University of Oxford were unsuccessful and CNAA validation was the only fall-back, offering limited institutional support necessary to sustain the College. While other colleges were able to diversify courses in higher education and expand numbers, Westminster became overly reliant on teacher education and theology as its main offerings, despite the amendment to the Trust Deed allowing such developments in 'further and higher education' in 1975. New courses and the development of in-service courses and opportunities in continuing education broadened the portfolio and helped to reduce the effect of over-reliance on teacher training but the institutional base still remained smaller than many of its main competitors in a shrinking market. From the late 1970s, a determined effort to expand the religious studies and theology areas capitalized on a niche in the market which fitted the church-relatedness of the College well.

To the Methodist Conference of 1979 came the report on conversations initiated by the College that 'there might be mutual benefit in merging a large proportion, numerically, of Ministerial Training' with the College.[47] The conclusion was reached by the Division of Ministries Board that such a merger was not advisable. It was a further fourteen years before the newly-established Wesley and Methodist Studies Centre at the College was regarded as able to deliver programmes suitable for ministerial training at different levels, though many Methodist ministers previously engaged in the College's Masters course in Applied (later Practical and Contextual) Theology, pioneered in the early 1980s for professional theological reflection in ministerial practice. Amongst its earliest graduates was Revd (now Dr) Inderjit Bhogal, of the Urban Theology Unit, Sheffield.

Under the principalship of Kenneth Wilson (1981–1997) advantage was taken of an upturn in student numbers in higher education, developing new courses and degrees in theology at access, undergraduate and postgraduate levels which led to the College being 'one of the largest centres of theological enquiry in the UK' by the mid-1990s.[48] The internationalization of the College proceeded apace, with the development of links with Europe through the ERASMUS programme, with American Methodist institutions and with partner educational institutions in South Africa and South East Asia. These were to help serve and understand 'Christian values, social justice, academic excellence, professional commitment and theological enquiry'.[49] This broadening of student and staff experience through exchange programmes was one aspect of the Principal's preoccupation with a wide and inclusive curriculum which enriched the quest for a fully human individual:

> We pay full attention to those values associated with a liberal education and the moral and spiritual perspectives which underpin our search for our humanity. An ability to ask questions fearlessly, to enjoy life wholeheartedly, to recognise one's responsibility to others are surely marks of the educated person to which every institution of higher learning should pay attention.[50]

The widening participation of groups under-represented in higher education was encouraged through the development of open learning programmes and provision of access to higher education for women and mature students, all marks of the inclusivity and desire to serve the disadvantaged which had characterized the College since its beginnings. The College was also seen as a scholarly community in which research as well as teaching should be encouraged. A number of research centres were established, notably in Religious Education, Special Educational Needs and Wesley and Methodist Studies.

From the mid-1980s to the mid-1990s the College experienced an unprecedented period of growth. Student numbers rose to a peak of 2,800 in 1996 (of which 1,173 were full-time students) but then suffered a calamitous decline with consequent financial pressures as student numbers slumped and short-term courses and consultancy failed to meet the targets needed to bridge the gap. The new relationship with the University of Oxford which agreed to validate courses in education and theology at undergraduate and postgraduate levels from 1992 brought some expansion of numbers initially but ultimately tied the hands of those who sought to diversify further. A new degree of B.A. in Humanities validated by the Open University turned out to be an unfortunate diversion from more deep-seated problems of recruitment in core activities. The warning given to the 1993 Methodist Conference proved to be prophetic: 'The world of education has entered the market place with a vengeance. Never has it been more important to maintain and develop the Christian community and values which have made Westminster College what it is.'[51]

The principalship of Richard Ralph (1997–2000) was preoccupied with the pain of coming to terms with declining numbers of students and the failure to generate sufficient income to meet the needs of a large campus requiring more capital expenditure on maintenance. This came at a time of increasing pressure on smaller institutions to make strategic alliances with others in order to gain greater stability. Faced with difficult choices, the Governing Body turned first to its validating body, the University of Oxford to explore ways in which immediate help might be found in facing the problem of declining numbers and impending financial crisis. These talks were unsuccessful. Further discussions led to a strategic alliance with Oxford Brookes University and merger in 2000, creating on the Harcourt Hill site the Westminster Institute of Education as a result of the move of the School of Education from Wheatley (formerly Lady Spencer Churchill College). This was seen as the best way in which the Methodist Church, leasing the site on a long-term basis to the University, could preserve opportunities for maintaining and developing the traditions of the College and its contribution to the training of teachers and to theological enquiry. The work of the Wesley and Methodist Studies Centre in the Institute was a guarantee of the continuing church-related work of the institution and the provision of Chaplaincy services, in conjunction with other colleagues in the Institute and wider University.

Conclusion

The quest for holiness, the Christian Perfection of which Wesley wrote, is as important today for education in the secular sphere as it is in the purely religious context. Wesley's experimental divinity was a holding together of the theoretical and the practical. The principle of faith working by love in service of God and neighbour was at the heart of his understanding of theology, the very essence of education, namely the Church as a learning community, in small groups and in larger institutions. John Scott, the first Principal of Westminster College reminded his staff and students that the College was about a religion of the heart just as much as of the mind. Relationships matter. Values (or virtues) matter — truth and honesty, friendship and compassion, justice and peace. The emphasis which we place on these things in our teaching and learning, in our social interaction, enables us to be distinctive as a church-related institution of higher education. Philip Budd's teaching in class and preaching in the College Chapel have brought that deep integration of the holy life and the critical faculties of reasoning and experience of life together in the service of not only generations of students at Westminster but also the wider world of biblical scholarship.

The Methodist Church has been challenged by the responsibility to provide students with a quality of education which is both rigorous and religious, which does not alienate them from the people they are called to serve, but which preserves the academic freedom of enquiry and scholarship, in an open and inclusive community where dialogue among people of faith (and no faith) and between disciplines can flourish and enrich human society. I suggest that what goes on here at the Westminster Institute of Education should not be consumer-led, driven by the whims of an increasingly materialistic and hedonistic society, but value-laden, seeking to transform society by its emphasis on the spiritual, moral, social and cultural values which we aim to convey. That is why I am glad to see such values at the heart of what goes on in church-related institutions. Wesley looks down and, I think, smiles approvingly at our critical reasoning, at the scholarship and excellence we promote in academic studies and sport and cultural activities, at the communication skills we develop, but above all at the real-world experiences which enable us all to connect the things we learn with the way we lead our lives and serve others in society. These things enable us to realize our full potential as children of God, in whatever vocation we follow, as teachers, as doctors or medical staff, as business people and as servants in the community. The partnership model means that we need each other: Church, Academy and Society. We particularly honour those who make possible the internationalizing of our programmes in the globalisation of our education. This makes the concept of global citizenship central to what we stand for and do at the beginning of the twenty-first century.

I finish with words written by Charles Wesley for the opening of Kingswood School, the first Methodist public school, in 1748:

Unite the pair long disjoined
Knowledge and vital piety:
Learning and holiness combined,
And truth and love, let all men see.
In those whom up to thee we give
Thine, wholly thine, to die and live.

Notes

1. Methodist Church Report, *The Essence of Education* (Peterborough: Methodist Publishing House, 1999), pp. 7–12.
2. R. E. Davies, *A Christian Theology of Education* (London: Denholm House Press, 1974), p. 33.
3. S. J. Hels, *Methodism and Education: From Roots to Fulfilment* (Nashville: General Board of Higher Education and Ministry, 2000), p. 17.
4. G. Mursell, *English Spirituality from 1700 to the Present Day* (London: SPCK, 2001), p. 88.
5. R. E. Davies, 'The Protestant Tradition in Education', *London Quarterly and Holborn Review* (1956), p. 258.
6. G. R. Osborn, 'Methodism and Education', *London Quarterly and Holborn Review* (1956), p. 259.
7. J. McDonald, 'An Address to the Preachers late in Connexion with the Rev J. Wesley: on the necessity and utility of establishing a plan, for securing to all the children of the Methodists, a regular CHRISTIAN EDUCATION' (Rochdale: J. Hartley, 1821), p. 3. To be found in the Wesley and Methodist Studies Centre at the Westminster Institute of Education, Oxford Brookes University.
8. Ibid., p. 35.
9. J. T. Smith, *Methodism and Education 1849–1902: J. H. Rigg, Romanism and Wesleyan Schools* (Oxford: Oxford University Press, 1998), p. 12.
10. I. C. Howard, *Controversies in Methodism over Methods of Education of Ministers up to 1836* (Unpublished thesis, University of Iowa, 1965), p. 160.
11. J. Entwistle, *Memoir of the Rev. Joseph Entwistle* (Bristol: N. Lomas, 1848), pp. 491–3. To be found in the Wesley and Methodist Studies Centre at the Westminster Institute of Education, Oxford Brookes University.
12. J. H. Rigg, 'The Christian Ministry', in *Discourses and Addresses on Leading Truths of Religion and Philosophy* (London: Wesleyan Conference Office, 1880), p. 168 and p. 177. See also T. Macquiban,

'Practical Piety or Lettered Learning', *Proceedings of the Wesley Historical Society*, 50 (1995–1996), pp. 83–107.

13. W. Vevers, 'An Essay on the National Importance of Methodism' (London: John Mason, 1831), p. 58. To be found in the Wesley and Methodist Studies Centre at the Westminster Institute of Education, Oxford Brookes University.

14. Smith, *Methodism and Education*, p. 17.

15. M. Arnold, *Reports on Elementary Schools 1852–1882* (London: HMSO, 1908), p. 231.

16. Wesleyan Education Committee (WEC) Report, 1865, p. 116. To be found in the Wesley and Methodist Studies Centre at the Westminster Institute of Education, Oxford Brookes University.

17. H. F. Matthews, *Methodism and the Education of the People 1791–1851* (London: Epworth Press, 1949), p. 129.

18. Wesleyan Education Committee Report, 1849, p. 12.

19. F. C. Pritchard, *The Story of Westminster College 1851–1952* (London: Epworth Press, 1951), p. 33.

20. J. Scott, 'Addresses to the Students of the Wesleyan Training Institution Westminster' (London: Wesleyan Training College, 1869), p. ix.

21. Ibid., p. 10 and p. 23.

22. Ibid., p. 36.

23. Ibid., p. 142.

24. Ibid., p. 67.

25. Ibid., p. 75.

26. Ibid., p. 120.

27. Ibid., p. 355.

28. Ibid., pp. 148–58.

29. Wesleyan Education Committee Report, 1869, p. 20.

30. J. H. Rigg, *The Relations of John Wesley and Wesleyan Methodism to the Church of England Investigated and Determined* (London: Longman, 1871), pp. 24–5.

31. Smith, *Methodism and Education*, pp. 101–102 and p. 232.

32. Ibid., p. 171.

33. Pritchard, *Story of Westminster*, p. 52.

34. Smith, *Methodism and Education*, p. 226.

35. Pritchard, *Story of Westminster*, p. 114.

36. Ibid., p. 159.

37. Westminster College Annual Report, 1951–1952. To be found in the Wesley and Methodist Studies Centre at the Westminster Institute of Education, Oxford Brookes University.
38. Anecdotal evidence from 1951 students at the Westminster Society Reunion, September 2001.
39. Westminster College Annual Report, 1952–1953.
40. Westminster College Annual Report, 1953–1954.
41. Westminster College Annual Report, 1959–1960.
42. Ibid.
43. Westminster College Annual Report, 1967–1969.
44. Westminster College Annual Report, 1963–1964.
45. Report on Westminster College in the Methodist Conference Agenda, 1971, p. 283.
46. Report on Westminster College in the Methodist Conference Agenda, 1973, p. 334.
47. Report on Westminster College in the Methodist Conference Agenda, 1979, p. 191.
48. Report on Westminster College in the Methodist Conference Agenda, 1994, p. 348.
49. Report on Westminster College in the Methodist Conference Agenda, 1990, p. 316.
50. Report on Westminster College in the Methodist Conference Agenda, 1994, p. 348.
51. Report on Westminster College in the Methodist Conference Agenda, 1993, p. 538.
52. F. Hildebrandt and O. A. Becherlegge (eds.), *A Collection of Hymns for the use of the People called Methodists* (Oxford: Clarendon Press, 1983), p. 643.

The Wisdom of Clouds: Religious Responses to Environmental Issues in the Blue Mountains of New South Wales

Richard Griffiths

'Who has put wisdom in the clouds, or given understanding to the mists?' (Job 38.36)

'Directly in front of me rose up the colossal bulk of Mt Solitary, shutting out a large part of the view down the valley. Around its base as the sun set there gradually rose up thin whisps of vapour like gauze clinging to its rocky sides as if loth to leave its shadow.' (Myles Dunphy)[1]

Introduction

The relationship between religion and the environment is highly complex. This is the case in Australia, at least as much as elsewhere.[2] This chapter seeks to delve into that complexity in the hope of uncovering what it might mean for environmentally sensitive religious practice to develop in a particular location – the Blue Mountains of New South Wales – and among the two most evident religions in the area – Christianity and Buddhism. It may be that certain features of this Australian experience serve to bring to clarity issues which are less obvious, or seemingly less pressing, elsewhere in the world.

Watching the clouds in the Jamieson Valley on his first visit to the Blue Mountains, west of Sydney, affected the course of Myles Dunphy's life. 'The air is so pure,' he wrote in his journal of that visit, 'it seems to annihilate space.'[3] It was his attraction to animate and inanimate nature that led him to pioneer the Australian bushwalking and conservation movements of the first half of the twentieth century. His vision in the 1920s for a national park to conserve the Blue Mountains finally came to fruition three quarters of a century later, with the creation of the Greater Blue Mountains World Heritage Area. It was in this landscape of looming sandstone cliffs and great forested valleys, of waterfalls cascading from heathy plateaux into deep gorges, that Dunphy found spiritual fulfilment. 'If you would find God,' he wrote in his personal journal, 'look to nature.'[4]

Although the Blue Mountains are best known for the bluish haze rising above vistas of eucalypt-filled valleys, edged with great rock faces, they are also well known, particularly by locals, for their mists. At a height of around a thousand metres, many days are cloudy, a feature noted in the literature of the region.[5] On the day these words are being written the upper Blue Mountains are blanketed with a thick mist, the sought-after views utterly obscured. Apart from myself, the only nature I can look to is the clouds. What form of wisdom could they possibly hold or withhold? The Buddha taught that one should indeed look to oneself. He told his disciples to look into their own minds as if into a clear sky. They reported back to him that all they could see there was clouds.[6] For many people it feels as though a relationship between religion and the environment ought to exist, yet it is unclear what that relationship actually is. The view from the perspective of a Western culture, which implicitly and explicitly discounts both categories, at the same time as strenuously maintaining their existence as distinct categories, is cloudy. Is an identification of the divine with the natural as straightforward as Dunphy supposed? Surely not, but then neither perhaps is the prospect necessarily as dim as the Buddha's followers feared.

In contemplating the clouds for which the Blue Mountains are well known it might be said that they represent a key dilemma in linking religion with the environment. On the one hand, the land and its associated flora, fauna and atmospheric effects – the entire ecosystem – are highly significant for life in the Blue Mountains (or anywhere else, for that matter). On the other hand, interpreting that significance is not an easy task. The clouds, and indeed whole ecosystems, can offer wisdom as to how humans might live sustainably in this place, but it is very difficult to read them in this way, very difficult to understand the ecological and spiritual wisdom they may have to offer.

Part of this difficulty is caused by the relatively short time people of non-Aboriginal descent have lived in the area. Hence there is a lack of accumulated wisdom about how to live in this particular place with a long-term perspective. This point has been brought home very recently by widespread bushfires burning beyond control in the lower Blue Mountains. These fires have acted in unprecedented ways, in terms of intensity, speed of spread and ability to jump large firebreaks and natural barriers, making it clear just how little non-indigenous society yet knows about the behaviour and characteristics of the land it inhabits.

In his controversial work *The Future Eaters* Tim Flannery argues that one of the key elements of human culture is 'the embodiment, in beliefs and customs, of actions that help people survive in their particular environment'.[7] He claims that the majority of the world's cultures are not attuned to their ecology because 'cultures that we can call "ecologically attuned", are the result of many thousands of years of experiencing and learning about a particular ecosystem'.[8] Cultural maladaptation, he argues, is particularly severe in Australia because it has a very high proportion of 'new' settlers, along with 'an extremely difficult and unusual ecology'.[9] Developing Flannery's hypothesis, it may be that Australia exhibits a degree of 'religious maladaptation' as part of its cultural heritage.

Another reason for the difficulty experienced in reading the ecological and religious significance of the clouds, the land, and the ecosystem is an ongoing reluctance to recognize and interpret the already existing meanings that have been inscribed there. David Malouf writes:

> The land had received the imprint of culture long before we came to it. It had been shaped by use and humanised by knowledge both practical and sacred ... What we did when we came here was lay new forms of knowledge and a new culture, a new consciousness, over so much that already existed.[10]

He points out that what was taken from indigenous Australians was largely not untouched nature, but 'a *made* nature, which we went on to make in *our* way'.[11]

Ultimately, then, if we are to read 'the wisdom of clouds' in a spiritually and culturally literate fashion, we will have to overcome these two obstacles. This would mean a recognition of the possibility of ecological maladaptation on the part of religions, along with a willingness to learn from Aboriginal traditions, even while acknowledging that much of value has already been lost, and that much, too, may remain 'untranslatable'.

Religion and Environmental Wisdom

If there is a conflict between Aboriginal and Western ways of knowing the land, there is also a conflict of knowledge *within* Western culture. In Western thought, humanity's relationship with its environment has increasingly been construed as a problem, or set of problems, demanding knowledge or wisdom to solve. Where this wisdom is to come from has been a matter for considerable debate, in which competing 'ways of knowing' have vied for supremacy, their respective advocates all laying claim to have answers to the perceived 'environmental crisis'. Science has tended to take centre stage as the chief means of knowing at our disposal; for us science, *scientia*, literally *is* knowledge. Since many environmental problems are known first and 'best' by scientific means (ozone depletion and the greenhouse effect to name but two, neither of which can be observed directly, but are rather the creations of scientific hypothesis), it seems self-evident that scientific knowledge is what will most readily offer the solutions.[12] This prioritizing of scientific wisdom as the only really relevant knowledge is as true within the environmental movement as it is in society at large. Hence the environmentalist and ecologist Paul Ehrlich writes:

> I am convinced that a quasi-religious movement, one concerned with the need to change the values that now govern much of human activity, is essential to the persistence of our civilisation. But agreeing that science, even the science of ecology, does not answer all questions – that there are "other ways of knowing" – does not diminish the absolutely critical role that good science must play if our over-extended civilization is to save itself.[13]

Those who have an interest in the possibility of religion as a way of knowing will note the distinctly half-hearted way in which Ehrlich concedes this possibility: although science may not be able to answer all questions, *quasi*-religious activity is presumably held by him to be better than the real thing; and perhaps with a nod to Foucault, the phrase "other ways of knowing" can only appear in print when safely surrounded by quotation marks, lest readers believe there *really are* ways of knowing other than, or complimentary to, the dominant scientific ones. Ironically, Ehrlich's point is grudgingly made in the context not of scientific observation but of soteriological anxiety: the hope that civilization will find the means to 'save itself'.

Less ambivalent than Ehrlich in its desire to see religious as well as scientific wisdom brought to bear on environmental concerns, is the following extract from a statement signed by sixteen hundred senior scientists including half of all living Nobel Prizewinners:

> As scientists, many of us have had profound experiences of awe and reverence before the universe. We understand that what is regarded as sacred is more likely to be treated with care and respect. Our planetary home should be so regarded. Efforts to safeguard and cherish the environment need to be infused with a vision of the sacred.[14]

This concern for the sacred as a valid way of perceiving reality, a valid form of knowledge, is unambivalent, but it retains a strong undercurrent of instrumentalism. The world is not necessarily *intrinsically* sacred. Rather it is because sacred objects tend to be respected that the world should be seen as such.

These attitudes are compounded by the often non-local, universalizing nature of both environmental and religious discourse. The grand narratives of global ecological doom, and of global religious salvation may well serve to alienate people from their particular experience of place. When it comes to the environment, this has the effect of making people aware of 'environmental issues' generally, but not of specific issues that affect their particular locality.[15] It may also act to inhibit people who profess religious faith to make conscious links between their (universal) beliefs and whatever (localized) environmental concerns they do experience.

European discourse on the nature of Australia has always been implicitly religious. The European name 'Australia' has a specifically religious origin. When the Spanish sailor and explorer Pedro Quiros landed in Vanuatu in 1605 he proclaimed the still undiscovered southern continent 'Terra Australis del Espiritu Santo' (The Great South Land of the Holy Spirit). According to Nicholas Coleman, 'Quiros saw Australia in a religious light and joyfully named it for the Holy Land he dreamed it could be.'[16]

The contemporary debates concerning land-use in Australia are no less religious in tone. In one of a series of national radio lectures, Australian author David Malouf said:

> There are many people in these last years for whom nature has become the last repository of the sacred. Saving it, saving every last scrap of it,

every species, every tree and plant, is a religious duty. The struggle between farmers and conservationists, loggers and conservationists, developers and conservationists, has become for them another and later version of the old fight between moral and spiritual purity on one hand and on the other the devil's work that is inherent in the day-to-day business of being in the world. Evangelical apocalyptic language, and a hectoring self-righteousness, powers their energy and gives shape to their arguments. The fervour is understandable and may even be necessary; but self-righteousness is not a pretty phenomenon.[17]

My argument here is that religion and the environment are fundamentally interlinked. Certainly, as Malouf points out, their discourses can be similar. However, it is more often the case that environmental arguments begin to sound religious than the other way around. Religious practice needs to be more aware of its ecological context if it is to hold vitality in people's lives. There is a need to adapt religion to biological reality, not vice versa. Religious discourse must develop an awareness of the ecological conditions of its own survival. Here in the Blue Mountains, biological reality is as imposing as it is inescapable. What then of the religious reality, and the connection between the two?

The Blue Mountains

The Blue Mountains lie between 60 and a 180 kilometres to the west of the Sydney metropolitan area in New South Wales and are made up of a deeply eroded sandstone plateau rising up to 1300m above sea level. There is material evidence that Aboriginal people have been living in the region for at least 14,000 years, evidence such as axe grinding grooves, rock engravings and charcoal and ochre drawings. European settlement only began in the early nineteenth century, as explorers sought a route from the Sydney coastal plain to the interior. The Blue Mountains are rich in biodiversity, with 13% of the world's eucalypt species found in the area and over 70 vegetation communities. There are 127 rare or threatened plant species and about 40 rare or threatened vertebrate animals. Reserves to protect the region began to be declared from the 1890s onwards, but since 1959 much of the area, over 270,000 hectares, has been protected in the Blue Mountains National Park, which itself connects to other protected areas: Wollemi, Yengo, Nattai, Kanangra-Boyd, Gardens of Stone and

Thirlmere Lakes National Parks, along with Jenolan Caves Karst Conservation Reserve. These eight protected areas form the 1.03 million hectare Greater Blue Mountains Area, which was accorded World Heritage status by UNESCO at the end of 2000.

The Blue Mountains National Park is bisected by a major transport and urban development corridor, with the Great Western Highway and the main railway line close against one another on a ridge of the plateau. This corridor threatens to compromise the ecological integrity of the National Park. The road follows roughly the same line as the first road across the Mountains, built in 1815. The railway line came later, in 1868. Along this corridor lie most of the twenty-six townships that form the City of the Blue Mountains, with a total population of around 72,500. The main township, Katoomba, is sited near one of Australia's most celebrated landmarks, a rock formation called the Three Sisters, a promontory of the main cliff face high above the floor of the Jamieson Valley. Such landmarks, with their associated lookout points and walking trails, have contributed to the ongoing popularity of the area as a major tourist destination, making the Blue Mountains National Park the most visited National Park in the country, and tourism a major economic sector. The area is symbolically important for the Australian conservation movement, as the main destination point for the early Sydney bushwalking groups and as the focus of attention of conservation pioneers such as Myles Dunphy, who famously helped to save the Blue Gum Forest in the Grose Valley from destruction.[18]

As much of the human population is centred on ridge-tops, drainage is largely to the north or the south, directly into the National Park. This area in particular is also subject to significant tourism impacts. Such population pressures result in the increased threat of weed invasion, pollution from sewage or nutrient enrichment from gardens and urban runoff, deliberate or accidental fires and sedimentation. Significant efforts are now underway to control further urban development and funds have been made available for the repurchase of private land. Efforts are also underway to make major improvements to sewage treatment.

Introduced species are a further significant problem, and are a major focus for management programmes. There are at least 39 plants classified as noxious under the 1993 Noxious Weeds Act which occur within the park. In the main these are localized to disturbed sites, particularly close to areas of human habitation. The inhabitants of such an environmentally sensitive region have ample opportunities to learn how they might lessen their impact on their surrounding ecology, such as through the Blue Mountains Conservation Society's widely available booklet, *Living in the Bush*. However, in most respects, life in the Blue Mountains is not significantly different from that lived elsewhere in Australia.

Religious Groups in the Blue Mountains

The most visible religion of the Blue Mountains, as of the rest of Australia, is Christianity, with the main Australian denominations all represented. The Blue Mountains Community Directory lists around fifty churches and a number of other Christian facilities such as conference centres. For most churches, environmental concerns are only one aspect of their work among many. One significant local feature of conservation activity, however, is protecting the heritage value of church grounds. For example, Leura Uniting Church has a garden adjoining its building which was designed by Paul Sorenson, the nationally famous Blue Mountains landscaper, who was a member of the church. This has recently been heritage listed by the City Council.

A noticeable local phenomenon is the incidence of Buddhist groups in the Mountains, which is more than four times the New South Wales average per head of the population (Australian Buddhist Directory). The Blue Mountains have a nationally significant recent history of Buddhist presence. In 1971 the Buddhist Society of New South Wales sponsored a Sri Lankan monk named Somaloka to reside at its retreat centre in Katoomba.[19] This became the first Buddhist monastery in Australia. Traditions represented at the start of the twenty-first century range from groups affiliated to 'Western' Buddhist organizations such as Insight Meditation and Friends of the Western Buddhist Order, to temples of ethnic Buddhist origin, such as Korean and Sri Lankan. Particularly in evidence is the small but growing influence of Tibetan Buddhism on Australian society, with four Tibetan groups present in the Blue Mountains.

Here there is space to examine only two religious groups in the Blue Mountains in any detail, one Christian, the other Buddhist. They have been chosen because of what they show of the religion/environment dilemma that I am depicting, and because they are fairly typical forms of religious organization, here and elsewhere.

1. Intelife (Mission Employment)

Intelife started in the early-1990s as acres of disused sandstone quarry on the edge of Wentworth Falls in the Blue Mountains. It took staff of Mission Employment in Katoomba eighteen months to put together a proposal to convert the quarry into something entirely different. Mission Employment is a part of Mission Australia, an association of the City Missions of a number of Australian state capitals. Although Christian based, Mission Employment aims to deliver employment opportunities and training for people regardless of their beliefs, and it is mainly funded by public monies. The idea was to convert the barren, scarred earth into a centre for demonstrating environmentally sensitive building, technology and lifestyles. Intelife aimed to incorporate crisis accommodation for homeless young people, as well as training facilities where long-term unemployed people could learn new skills. Along the way, both unemployed and homeless young people gained skills while helping create the infrastructure of the project. Supervising staff on site gave skill training where possible, with qualified tradespeople brought in to instruct on specialized tasks. A number of groups have made use of the training facilities of the project, including Greencorps, an environmental employment scheme for young adults.

Intelife began formally in 1994, with grants from a number of corporate sponsors, including Levi Strauss, and the donated design services of a Sydney-based architect to create state-of-the-art environmentally sensitive buildings. These incorporated passive and active solar design, with a photovoltaic system donated by the power company Integral Energy. The site's waste water system was designed and monitored by the University of Western Sydney water research laboratory. Intelife has spawned a similar project in Penrith, western Sydney, also run by Mission Employment, and has itself been undergoing reorganization. It remains to be seen where its future lies.

2. Vajrasattva Mountain Centre

Vajrasattva Mountain Centre was established in the mid-1990s at the instigation of Lama Zopa Rinpoche, a disciple of the Dalai Lama, under the auspices of the Foundation for the Preservation of the Mahayana Tradition. As such, it is fairly typical of the many Tibetan Buddhist centres that have sprung up in the West since the Chinese takeover of Tibet. The centre operates out of a modest converted residential house on a prominent street in Katoomba. It currently has thirty members, and a larger number who offer less formal support.

The director of this meditation and cultural centre of the Gelug tradition is Norma Brahatis, a lay Buddhist who was born in the Blue Mountains and has lived there for more than fifty years. In her view Tibetan Buddhists have a particular traditional concern for the protection of their beautiful and fragile country. The Bodhisattva vows that Buddhists take commit them to avoid harming sentient beings. They also influence where one lives and how one interacts with other living things. In particular, the eighteenth root vow forbids 'destroying any town or country, such as by fire, bombs, pollution, black magic, and so forth'.[20] Contemporary interpretations of this vow include consideration of environmental concerns. Overall an attitude of 'the deepest respect' for sentient beings is cultivated. The Mountain Centre looks to the teachings of the Dalai Lama in relation to the environment. The Dalai Lama has proved expert at relating his ancient religious tradition to modern Western concerns.

For local Buddhists, an important factor is that the Blue Mountains are considered a pristine environment, clear and clean. As such it is perceived as being a good place for the mind to reflect. Further than this, a number of the Centre's members are involved in bushcare activities.[21] A current project of the Centre is the building of a stupa as a witness for world peace.

Analysis

1. Religion as an impediment to environmental sensitivity

The Vajrasattva Mountain Centre is typical of the situation of many local assemblies of religious practitioners. Although ritual and teaching certainly seem to support the environmentalist activities of those adherents who already have a passion for environmental concerns, there is little emphasis, either in the teachings themselves, or in the physical infrastructure of the group (buildings, land) on environmental concerns as a central or irreducible aspect of religious faith. There is no physical evidence in the Centre's buildings of any practical attempts to exist sustainably, or at least no evidence of any discrepancy between the Centre's practical environmental concern and that of any other group in society at large. This is obviously the case with religious buildings generally in the West, and the Blue Mountains is no exception. One might ask at this point whether religious organizations *should* necessarily 'lead the field' when it comes to such matters as the sustainable design of buildings. The point I am making is that if they do not, then they may be categorized as one facet of what Flannery calls 'cultural maladaptation', which inevitably calls into question the truth claims they may make. In other words, I am asserting that religious truth claims, as with any other form of human knowledge, should be tested against their ecological impact. The measure of religious truth is, at least, its impact on the natural environment in which that truth seeks to exist. As one former Buddhist environmentalist has claimed:

> What seems to happen to some 'Green Buddhists' is that Buddhism threatens to become your whole world, it is so all-embracing. The practices are demanding of time and energy, and the teachings pull you in deeper. Some of the practices, such as the Vajrasattva purification, involve holding your greatest enemies in unconditional positive regard, and enveloping the environment in healing light. This can act to transform or dissipate outrage at environmental injustice.[22]

In short, as religious faith becomes central, environmental activism may become marginal. Moreover, this is probably no less true of other religions than of Buddhism.

The Intelife project is fairly typical of activity with a religious basis, but which operates outside the orbit of a particular local religious community. Many para-church organizations manage to do worthwhile and often pioneering social work 'on behalf of' the church. However, it is not clear that their activities have a great deal of impact on the beliefs or behaviour of grass-roots believers, even on those in the immediate vicinity of the particular project. Projects such as Intelife can appear to 'ordinary' believers as marginal or irrelevant to the central concerns of faith, and can fairly easily be labelled 'eccentric'. It is hard to find immediate links between the environmental values evidenced by Intelife and those of local Christian communities. Those who work in such projects live with a dilemma, since it is often only outside the local church that activity of this sort can develop. However, as the story of Intelife shows, its marginal position in relation to the church makes it highly vulnerable to changes of outside funding, public policy and political support.

2. Religion as land management

On the whole, land management is seen as an inessential part of those religions that have been imported to Australia during the last two centuries. For instance, while the established churches are often in fact major land-owners, this is usually seen as a means to an end, and not in any sense as a religious end in itself. This is in contrast to indigenous pre-European forms of land management, which were inherently 'religious' in character. Nicholas Coleman writes:

> The land calls on Aborigines to cooperate with the creative cycle. Only that way can the land fulfil its own creative destiny. The country cares for those who belong to it, by sustaining their lives; and those who belong to the country care for it, through ceremony and land management ... Human caring of the highest order for the land has the quality and status of ceremony ... On a more pragmatic yet nonetheless religious level, care for the country entails keeping it 'clean' (fire management), a cautious use of its resources, observing totemic taboos (for instance leaving reserves for species near their sacred sites), and educating the young to carry on the tradition of caring.[23]

It is of course dangerous to generalize about or to romanticize Aboriginal spirituality. Nor is it necessarily appropriate to depict it as a kind of 'green' religion. To do so would say more about our own preoccupations than about reality. However, what Coleman's claim, quoted above, contributes to the present discussion is an indication of just how far Buddhists, Christians and other faith communities have to go before they can be considered 'native to this place', able to exist sustainably within the confines of an exacting ecology. The Vajrasattva Mountain Centre is able to promote views that *may* lead to sustainable land use practices, but these do not substantially affect its own operating. On the other hand, the Intelife project is able to embody a more sustainable approach to land use, but it cannot (or does not want to) bridge the gap between environmental practice and the theological interpretation of that practice by local Christian communities.

Conclusion

I have attempted to explore in a preliminary fashion the idea of religious practice as a form of relationship with the land, a dynamic relationship between the community of religious practitioners and the ecosystems in which they exist. I have shown that typically, such a relationship is highly tenuous, leading to the suggestion that much of contemporary religion may be regarded as 'environmentally maladapted'. In doing so I have limited the discussion to one fairly small and unique area. This is deliberate. If religious practice is to be a valid form of environmental knowledge it must be local not universal, concrete not abstract, activist not quietist, a relationship with the land that in the context of traditional agriculture David Malouf calls 'an entirely different form of science: the knowledge that comes from tradition and the questioning of tradition, by trial and error, on the ground'.[24]

The environmental sensitivities of the Blue Mountains, influenced as they are by an internationally important ecosystem and by the often hard realities of an economy based on tourism, remain resolutely unique and particular to one place on earth. Religion, like land management, must pay attention to the reality of the place, with all its opportunities and limitations. In their work of environmental history, *Topsoil and Civilisation*, Vernon Carter and Tom Dale write, 'civilised man [sic] has consistently tried to make the land fit his pattern of farming, when he should make the farming fit the pattern of the land'.[25] What they say of farming should surely now be said of religious activity. The task in the Blue Mountains, and perhaps elsewhere, is to allow religious faith to fit the pattern of the land, this great Southern Land of the Holy Spirit. However, contrary to the approach of conventional agriculture which objectifies land as a resource alone, the land is not the mere object of religious practice, but its subject. As the Catholic priest and self-styled 'geologian', Thomas Berry writes:

> The natural world is subject as well as object ... The natural world is the larger sacred community to which we belong. To be alienated from this

community is to become destitute in all that makes us human. To damage this community is to diminish our own experience.[26]

The kind of well-adapted interaction between religion and the environment I am suggesting is well-envisioned by the Christian farmer and poet Wendell Berry, as quoted by the Buddhist environmentalist, Joanna Macy:

> If we will have the wisdom to survive,
> to stand like slow growing trees
> on a ruined place, renewing, enriching it ...
>
> then a long time after we are dead
> the lives our lives prepare will live
> here, their houses strongly placed upon the valley sides ...
> The river will run
> clear, as we will never know it ...
>
> On the steeps where greed and ignorance cut down
> the old forest, an old forest will stand,
> its rich leaf-fall drifting on its roots.
> The veins of forgotten springs will have opened.
> Families will be singing in the fields ...
>
> Memory,
> native to this valley, will spread over it
> like a grove, and memory will grow
> into legend, legend into song, song
> into sacrament. The abundance of this place,
> the songs of its people and its birds,
> will be health and wisdom and indwelling
> light. This is no paradisal dream.
> Its hardship is its reality [sic].[27]

Notes

1. M. Dunphy, *Selected Writings* (Sydney: Ballagirin, 1986), p. 119.
2. Philosophical phenomenologists such as Neil Evernden consider that the word 'environment' is itself part of the problem. See his book *The Natural Alien: Humankind and Environment* (Toronto: University of Toronto Press, 1993). Thinking of an environment out there encourages us to think in terms of objects: the environment is construed as a separate thing or collection of things to save, rather than an intrinsic part of our existence. But according to Evernden, 'Environmentalism in the deepest sense is not about the environment. It is not about things, but relationships, not about being, but Being, not about the world, but about the inseparability of self and circumstance.' p.142.
3. *Selected Writings*, p. 119.
4. Ibid.
5. Delia Falconer's novel, *The Service of Clouds* (Sydney: Picador, 1997), is one such example.
6. Conversation with Norma Brahatis, Vajrasattva Mountain Centre, February 2002.
7. T. Flannery, *The Future Eaters. An Ecological History of the Australasian Lands and People* (Chatswood, NSW: Reed Books, 1994), p. 389.
8. Ibid.
9. Ibid., p. 390.
10. D. Malouf, *A Spirit of Play. The Making of Australian Consciousness*. Boyler Lectures 1998 (Sydney: ABC Books, 1998), p. 49 and p. 51.
11. Ibid., p. 49.
12. On the other hand, a large scale natural phenomenon such as El Nino Southern Oscillation (ENSO) has been 'known' about and compensated for by the peoples of Australia for generations before it was described in a scientifically acceptable manner in the early 1980s. See Flannery, *The Future Eaters*, p. 81.
13. P. Ehrlich, *The Machinery of Nature*, cited in D. Suzuki, *The Sacred Balance. Rediscovering our Place in Nature* (St Leonards, NSW: Allen &

Unwin, 1997), p. 27.

14. Union of Concerned Scientists, 'World Scientists Warning to Humanity', 18th Nov 1992, cited in Suzuki, *Sacred Balance*, p. 27.

15. See the opinion poll commissioned by the Australian Conservation Foundation shortly before the 2001 Federal election: *Attitudes to Environmental Issues in Four Electorates. Voter Attitudes in the Federal Electorates of Adelaide, La Trobe, Moreton and Richmond. Conducted for the ACF by Irving Saulwick and Associates* (Melbourne: Australian Conservation Federation, 2001). This found that while the majority of voters in four marginal electorates agreed that the environment was 'very important' or 'fairly important' as a political issue that would affect their voting preference, far fewer could name even a single specific environmental issue of recent concern to them. The analysis of the poll commented, 'The importance people attach to the environment as an issue appears to be based on principle rather than on the front-of-mind presence of specific environmental issues.' p. 4.

16. N. G. Coleman, *The Worlds of Religion* (Roseville, NSW: McGraw Hill, 1999), p. 15.

17. Malouf, *Spirit of Play*, pp. 56–7.

18. A. Macqueen, *Back from the Brink. Blue Gum Forest and the Grose Wilderness* (Springwood, NSW: Andy Macqueen, 1997).

19. E. Adam and P. J. Hughes, *The Buddhists in Australia* (Canberra: Australian Government Publishing Service, 1996), pp. 9–10.

20. Foundation for the Preservation of the Mahayana Tradition, *The Bodhisattva Vows*, 2nd edn. (Kathmandu, Nepal: Kopan Monastery, 1997), p. 5.

21. Croucher's history of Australian Buddhism notes the early connection between Buddhist practice and what might be termed 'proto-environmentalism'. 'Australian Buddhists were often interested in other rationalist and humanitarian causes, such as conservation, bushwalking and vegetarianism.' H. M. Carey, *Believing in Australia. A Cultural History of Religions* (St Leonards, NSW: Allen & Unwin, 1996), p. 150, citing P. Croucher, *A History of Buddhism in Australia. 1848–1988* (Sydney: UNSWP, 1989), pp. 59–79.

22. J. Cameron, 'Place Perspective, Buddhism and Environmentalism' (University of Western Sydney Social Ecology Research Group E-Library, 1999).

[http://www.uws.edu.au/serg/Buddhismenv_jcameron.htm. Accessed 21.1.02]

23. Coleman, *Worlds of Religion*, pp. 49–50.
24. Malouf, *Spirit of Play*, p. 45.
25. Cited in Suzuki, *Sacred Balance*, p. 99.
26. T. Berry, *The Dream of the Earth* (San Francisco, CA: Sierra Club Books, 1988), cited in Suzuki, *Sacred Balance*, p. 240.
27. W. Berry, 'Work Song Part 2: A Vision', quoted in J. Macy, 'To the Limits of our Longing', *Permaculture International Journal*, 63 (1997), p. 37.

Divine Wisdom: A Discourse of Christian Feminist Theology

Angie Pears

Introduction

The encounter between feminisms and Christianity has shaped key aspects
of western Christian theological engagement over the last thirty years.
Regardless of which perspective is taken on the value and relevance of
feminist analysis and insights for Christianity, recognition needs to be given
to the often radical implications of this encounter for Christian theology
and practice. Many aspects of Christian practice and reflection have been
subject to detailed and rigorous feminist-informed investigation, including,
for example, god-language, imagery, organization, historical traditions,
influential theological texts, and of course the biblical traditions which
stand at the centre of Christian faith and understanding. Given such a
vital encounter between theology and feminisms there have been many
attempts to evaluate the theological impact and implications of feminisms
for Christian belief and practice. However, the historical patterns of the
development of Christian feminist theologies are such that studies have
tended to focus on responding to the fundamental but often devastating
feminist critique of Christianity as 'patriarchal' and oppressive to women,
and, most importantly, as intrinsically incompatible with feminist values
and visions. The binary differential between feminisms as compatible with
Christianity and feminisms as incompatible with Christianity has dominated
Christian feminist theologies and critical evaluation of these theologies.
Inevitably, perhaps, evaluative critique of Christian feminist and womanist
positions has often entailed or been motivated by the assertion of one

religious feminist perspective over another and this has diverted attention away from crucial detailed critical work. In short, critical energy has been taken up with the complex and demanding issue of the compatibility of feminism and Christianity. The result of this preoccupation was, until very recently, a clear lack of critical evaluative study focusing on the methodological mechanisms by which Christian theologies are informed by feminist values and critique.

As studies of the often dynamic relationship between feminisms and religion develop, however, of increasing concern is the identification and exploration of ways in which Christian feminist theologies are informed, sustained and made possible by feminist values and critiques. The imperative for detailed theological evaluation that marks out the methodological processes of the engagement of feminisms and Christianity becomes increasingly significant as the presence of feminisms in Christian theologies not only persists but also actually increases and diversifies. Evidence for both the beginnings of such evaluation and the impact and significance this evaluation might bring for feminist theological discourse comes with the 1997 collection *Horizons in Feminist Theology* edited by Rebecca Chopp and Sheila Greeve Davaney. This text marks the emergent questioning of the theoretical identity and perspectives of feminist theologies along with recognition of the ambiguous status of such questioning in terms of its reception and place in feminist theorizing. Critical evaluation now needs to move on from the question of the compatibility of Christianity and feminisms to identify and assess the types and success of particular strategies that have been developed by different Christian theologians to enable the creative encounter of feminisms and Christianity to take place. As part of this, a diverse range of motivations and perspectives needs to be recognized as resourcing and shaping feminist theologies.

Questions are increasingly being asked about the nature and workings of the critical relationship between two very different, but in some ways very similar, perspectives facilitating creative and often radical dialogue. By asking such questions it is possible to identify certain theological approaches and methodological mechanisms that characterize the facilitation of such dialogue in Christian feminist theologies. These mechanisms that have been employed variously by theologians enable them to accept the values and critiques of feminism, sometimes on a quite radical level, whilst at the same time proclaiming commitment to

Christianity. The task of assessing the 'effectiveness' of various methods and approaches that have been employed to facilitate such feminist Christian dialogue is crucial to understanding the ways in which feminist Christian encounter in its great diversity informs contemporary Christian theology. This now stands as a key task for contemporary theological analysis concerned with the interdependent relationship between Christian theology, culture and society.

Biblical Traditions and Feminist Theology

Given the authoritative place of biblical traditions in Christian theology and practice, critical evaluative engagement with the Bible has been a major part of Christian feminist theological discourse since the explicit address of Christian theology to feminist critique and insights. For many highly influential theologians who have contributed to the development and self-understanding of Christian feminist theologies, analysis of the ways in which biblical texts have been employed in the understanding and representation of gender and sexuality has proved crucial. So has the concern to explore new possibilities for interpreting and engaging biblical texts in a way that supports and reflects the perceived liberative emphases of feminisms.

For example, turning back to the earliest explicit traces of feminist theological analysis in the first wave of the women's movement in the nineteenth century, the work of Elizabeth Cady Stanton demonstrates the significance of the critical analysis of the history and possibilities of biblical texts for understanding and determining the societal status of women. Cady Stanton was an activist who was involved with planning the first women's rights convention in 1848 at Seneca Falls, New York. She was committed to opposing perceived inequalities of women's lives and as part of this identified the particular significance of the Bible which she argued had been used as a tool to silence and marginalize women. In many ways her work anticipated the extensive critical feminist hermeneutics that have been such a shaping and highly visible aspect of the challenging presence of feminism in Christian theology over the last thirty years. In the two-volume work, *The Woman's Bible*, that emerged in 1895 and 1898 Cady Stanton drew on contemporary insights of biblical scholarship and engaged in the systematic exegesis of biblical texts from a consciously woman-identified stance. She based her approach on the critical recognition of the very negative ways in which the Bible has been employed and in particular she was concerned to highlight and challenge the way in which the authoritative acclaim with which the Bible was held by Christians had been used as a tool of androcentric interpretation and to justify a theology which asserted the subjugation of women:

> From the inauguration of the movement for women's emancipation the Bible has been used to hold her in the "divinely ordained sphere", prescribed in the Old and New Testaments … The Bible teaches that woman brought sin and death into the world, that she precipitated the fall of the race, that she was arraigned before the judgement seat of Heaven, tried, condemned and sentenced. Marriage for her was to be a condition of bondage, maternity a period of suffering and anguish, and in silence and subjugation, she was to play the role of a dependent on man's bounty for all her material wants, and for all the information she might desire on the vital questions of the hour, she was commanded to ask her husband at home. Here is the Bible's position of woman briefly summed up.[1]

For scholars like Cady Stanton, given the status and the role of the Bible in the Christian faith, a central feminist task has to be the critical address to the ways in which the Bible has been used. This has led to the discovery of a variety of mechanisms by which texts can be approached and assessed in terms of their functioning and liberative possibilities. Just as certain mechanisms or approaches have been developed to facilitate this critical work, so certain texts or particular themes and concepts have emerged as central foci to this work. For example, the four Gospels, the writings of Paul and Genesis have become key texts in understanding and exploring feminist Christian possibilities. Key themes and traditions here include the development of the early Church, the prophetic tradition, and, more recently, the traditions of divine wisdom with a particular focus placed on the biblical wisdom traditions. Texts of significance include Proverbs, Ecclesiastes, Job, the Song of Songs, the apocryphal books of Sirach and the Wisdom of Solomon, and the four Gospels. In particular, the feminist theological focus on divine wisdom has been concerned with the development of feminist spirituality which employs the biblical resources of the figure and traces of wisdom variously expressed as Sophia, Shekhina or Chokmah.

Over the last few years a number of important publications have illustrated the way in which divine wisdom is emerging as an important and versatile aspect of feminist Christian engagement. See for example, Elisabeth Schüssler Fiorenza, *Jesus: Miriam's Child, Sophia's Prophet* (1995), Athalya Brenner and Carole Fontaine (eds.), *Wisdom and Psalms: A Feminist Companion to the Bible* (1998), and Maria Pilar Aquino and Elisabeth Schüssler Fiorenza (eds.), *In the Power of Wisdom: Feminist Spiritualities of Struggle* (2000). *In the Power of Wisdom* is an important collection as it engages the traditions and possibilities of divine wisdom in a variety of social, political and religious contexts to develop feminist-informed spiritualities of struggle. In the collection, for example, are articles by Nami Kim who explores spiritualities of struggle in Korean society, Susan Starr Sered who focuses on Jewish feminism and the Shekhina, and Mary Condren who focuses on Catholicism in Ireland and Celtic religion. Elisabeth Schüssler Fiorenza captures something of the radical possibilities envisaged in the traditions of divine wisdom by feminists in her editorial comment:

> The individual articles probe the possibilities for articulating a political Wisdom spirituality that sustains rather than mutes struggles for survival and liberation. The contributions focus on religious resources for such a spirituality and centre on issues of sacred power and justice. They articulate a spiritual vision that not only expresses wo/men's struggles to survive and transform relations of domination but also critically identifies religious traditions and resources for such a discernment of the Spirit-Shekhina-Sophia's working in different global contexts.[2]

Wisdom Literature and Orthodoxy

This focus on wisdom literature and traditions increasingly found in Christian feminist theologies is one important way in which Christian feminist encounter has employed radical feminist-informed mechanisms to explore the impact of gender-based imagery and language used for God in the biblical texts. It demonstrates the way in which radical critical tools of analysis and reconstruction have been developed by feminist theologians and employed in such a way as to claim a clear base in the traditions of Christian theology and practice. As with all of the texts and traditions that have been subject to such constant critical attention, questions need to be asked as to why this particular tradition is proving such an important resource for feminists who are attempting to identify and recover potentially liberative aspects of the Christian tradition that might be used to support and inform a feminist spirituality or religiosity. One reason for this is, as Silvia Schroer points out, the identification of divine wisdom as 'a female figure who is immediately associated with Israel's God and who advances a divine claim'.[3] From this radical possibilities are perceived for the functioning of divine wisdom in relation to the biblical images for God:

> Sophia, as an authentic biblical image of God, offers remarkable possibilities for breaking up the petrifactions and ontologizations of androcentric God language, and for doing so on the basis of a Jewish tradition. Her attributes are the attributes of God; when she speaks, God speaks; what she proclaims and does is God's will. She is the "wholly other," yet she makes herself known.[4]

This quest for female representations and traces of female links to the divine, and for female language used in relation to the divine, is found throughout feminist theological engagement. For example, one of the characterizing features of goddess thealogy is the reconstructive search to locate and engage symbols and traditions of the past and often such activity has been open to accusations of historical inaccuracy. However, the task is often understood by those involved as an explicit attempt to address perceived processes of marginalization and silencing in a creative and constructive way. In Christian feminist theologies the combination of radical reconstructive methodology and an appeal to 'orthodoxy' is a constant feature of feminist Christian encounter.

William Abraham in *Canon and Criterion in Christian Theology: From the Fathers to Feminism* (1998), for example, highlights the role that canon and an interest in canon have played in contemporary Christian feminist theology. He argues that despite expectations and some initial reading, the notion of canon lies at the heart of feminist theological activity, and that within such activity comes the potential for reconsidering approaches to Scripture and canon:

> Buried in the debate evoked by feminist criticism lies the possibility of developing a much more adequate interpretation of canon ... Feminist theologians have stumbled on to a vision of canon which has been long lost in the theories of the West ... The crucial concern which governs

feminist interest in Scripture initially is that any relevant canon must be a means of liberation. We might say that this is a fundamental conception of canon which governs the initial approach of feminist theology to Scripture.[5]

Abraham recognizes just how important the feminist work in this area is:

> The challenge to the Christian tradition posed by this stream of feminist criticism can be expressed in this fashion. Does the complex canonical heritage of the Church, when it is rightly used, provide healing for the sins of patriarchy and androcentricism? This is not an epistemological issue. Translating it into an epistemological problem merely ensures that its resolution will be dependent on the addressing of philosophical questions which yet await an adequate answer. It is a soteriological and moral problem, one of the many problems which the Christian tradition has had to resolve in its long pilgrimage throughout history.[6]

Traditions and sacred texts are engaged, then, but not without a radical hermeneutic of suspicion and a creative approach towards the recovery and contextualization of such traditions and texts.

The details of how the feminist focus on divine wisdom functions as a tool of feminist Christian encounter become clearer when critical analysis moves from general observations to a more located and particular evaluation in the work of Elisabeth Schüssler Fiorenza. Schüssler Fiorenza's contribution to the development and self-understanding of feminist theologies is outstanding. Her theological work has been at the forefront of biblical feminist hermeneutics and reconstruction. Schüssler Fiorenza argues that wisdom has become a resource for 'articulating a political Wisdom spirituality that sustains rather than mutes struggles for survival and liberation'.[7] What is of interest here is the way in which the wisdom tradition has been identified and then taken and emphasized as a resource for struggle today. In her earlier work, a similar pattern of critical feminist engagement is evident in Schüssler Fiorenza's approach to what she has termed the 'discipleship of equals', where she proposed a radical reconstructionist approach to the recovery and elaboration of women's Christian history and heritage. As part of the argument that she has forwarded for both the legitimacy and possibility of a Christian feminist theology, Schüssler Fiorenza has stressed that women's history and experience must not only be remembered but also that they must be reclaimed as women's own. Within the context of her own approach and detailing of continued Christian commitment in the face of the radical critique of feminism, this stress on heritage is particularly important. She is concerned not to give up women's Christian past too easily, and argues that post-traditional feminist theology often reinforces the idea that women did not have a significant role to play in the development of early Christianity, an interpretation that she rejects. For Schüssler Fiorenza the continuing influence of biblical religion on many women's lives is reason enough for giving serious critical address to the contribution of women to the early Christian movement:

> Insofar as biblical religion is still influential today, a cultural and social feminist transformation of Western society must take into account the biblical story and the historical impact of the biblical tradition. Western women are not able to discard completely and forget our personal, cultural, or religious Christian history. We will either transform it into a new liberating future or continue to be subject to its tyranny whether we recognize its power or not … Feminists cannot afford such an ahistorical or antihistorical stance because it is precisely the power of oppression that deprives people of their history.[8]

The recovery of women's biblical heritage stands at the centre of Schüssler Fiorenza's understanding of Christian feminist theological work: 'Relinquishing our biblical heritage merely reinforces the androcentric reality construction of Western culture according to which male existence and history is the paradigm of human existence and human history.'[9]

Fundamental to her approach is her critical understanding that the recording and transmission of biblical texts and traditions has supported and so perpetuated androcentric experience, an interpretation she claims is supported by historical-critical scholarship.[10] Behind this claim is an insight that characterizes feminist theological understanding that all theology is situated and interested. This challenges interpretations of theology as objective, universally valid and 'true', and stresses that theology, and indeed all scholarship, is inherently contextual. This claim was first explicitly articulated by Valerie Saiving in an article entitled 'The human situation: a feminine view' which was published in 1960 in *The Journal of Religion*.[11] The significance of this piece for understanding the development and methodological identity of feminist theologies is evident in reflections on the text by contemporary feminist theologians. It has been described by both Ursula King and Grace Jantzen as a 'landmark'[12] and by Daphne Hampson as 'the article which is often taken to mark the beginning of the current wave of feminist theological writing'.[13] In many ways Saiving's article is heralded as the beginning of contemporary feminist theological discourse. The style and content of Saiving's article, along with subsequent theological engagement with the kind of issues she raised, proved to be a definitive breakthrough in feminist theological engagement, and this is despite the fact that at the time her article received very little recognition or acclaim.

One of the most significant aspects of Saiving's analysis in 'The human situation' is her identification of the theological significance of differentiating between male and female experience (which she termed 'masculine' and 'feminine' experience). She posited as problematic the traditionally accepted generic use of the term 'men' by theologians and explored anthropological studies of the cultural influences of differences between male and female experiences such as Margaret Mead's *Male and Female* and Ruth Benedict's *Patterns of Culture*.[14] Drawing on such works Saiving located in the mother-child relationship, exclusive to women, a key formative role in establishing differentiated female and male identity. Reproductive capability is fundamental to Saiving's ideas about differences between male and female, and she refers to female identity in terms of 'being' and male identity in terms of 'becoming'.[15] She claimed that contemporary theology 'is not adequate to the universal human situation';[16] it does not allow women to be 'both women *and* full human beings'.[17] From this, she argues for a discernible difference between female and male experiences of sin, and specifically of what she claimed was women's tendency to servitude, and dependency for identity on others. In terms of the development of Christian feminist theologies, Saiving's understanding of the theological implications of differentiating between male and female experiences is significant here. Saiving's analysis is based on the fundamental insight that it is male experience that informs and shapes our understanding of reality, the human situation, and the conviction that a very different understanding would emerge if female experience were part of this shaping process:

> Saiving's essay, a landmark in feminist theology, was ten years ahead of its time … Saiving set forth what was to become the basic premise of all

feminist theology: that the vision of the theologian is affected by the particularities of his or her experience as male or female.[18]

Saiving articulates a fundamental feminist epistemological concern about the perception and naming of reality and compounds this concern with the insight that traditional namings, theological and doctrinal, are inadequate for both women and men. Unacknowledged gendered perceptions and linguistics lead to a partial theology of exclusion and privilege. It is important to note here that even at this very early stage of feminist theological analysis there is the crucial recognition that traditional theology and its underlying assumptions were detrimental and limiting not only for women but for men as well. The challenge of Saiving's work here is to Christian theological formation, as her analysis focused not so much on the historical and biblical traditions of inequality but on the nature and processes of theological reflection. Specifically, the insight of Saiving that has proved fundamental to Christian feminist theological methodology ever since and has in fact become almost foundational to such methodology, is the recognition of the gendered nature of experience and the striking implications that this has for theology.

The feminist critical response to a reading of theology as experientially based, and as traditionally male, is one that requires a certain degree of creative rewriting based in feminist consciousness. This is articulated clearly by Schüssler Fiorenza who has argued that the task of the feminist critical approach is not simply a case of straightforward retrieval, but rather it 'can be likened to the work of a detective insofar as it does not rely solely on historical "facts" nor invents its evidence, but is engaged in an imaginative reconstruction of historical reality'.[19] This, then, makes the reconstructive task both critical and creative: 'In the attempt to make the past intelligible the historian must go beyond the events in an act of "intellectual re-creation".'[20]

Schüssler Fiorenza employs this understanding and criterion of recovery to the traditions of divine wisdom and reflects the depth of the problem posed by the processes of recording and transmission that such traditions have been subject to. Her concern is to develop an approach which will enable the traditions of divine wisdom to be imaginatively reconstructed so that they might become a resource in the feminist theological task of overcoming injustice in its many forms and articulating alternative Christian discourses: 'How can we reconstitute this tradition in such a way that the rich table of Sophia can provide food and drink, nourishment and strength in the struggles for transforming Kyriarchy?'[21]

Schüssler Fiorenza traces the development of the wisdom traditions from Jewish literature to early Christian literature and attempts to address the apparent absence of the figure of divine wisdom in early Christian literature. She argues that despite this lack of visibility of the tradition an attentive, discerning approach to biblical texts will discover, 'that a submerged theology of Wisdom, or sophialogy, permeates all of Christian Scriptures. Early Jewish discourses on Divine Wisdom provided a theological linguistic matrix that was activated by early Christian communities'.[22]

In articulating the task facing Christian feminist theologians here she draws on Adrienne Rich's analysis of feminists as miners, digging and searching for traces and evidence of this tradition. One criticism of such an approach, and a criticism that has been levelled particularly at such selective reconstructive methodologies, is that it is in effect essentialist or neo-orthodox. Schüssler Fiorenza is concerned to stress that her own approach is not designed to simply locate, recover and then revere the core tradition of Christianity acceptable to feminists. Rather, 'I want to explore how feminist critical interpretations challenge the whole Christian community to engage in theological struggles to find appropriate language about the divine.'[23]

For Schüssler Fiorenza, then, the tradition of divine wisdom is appropriated and justifiably engaged in a critical constructive search. In *Jesus: Miriam's Child, Sophia's Prophet* Schüssler Fiorenza writes, 'By naming Jesus as the child of Miriam and the prophet of Divine Sophia, I seek to create a "women" – defined feminist theoretical space that makes it possible to dislodge christological discourses from their malestream frame of reference.'[24]

In identifying the early Christian discourse of divine wisdom Schüssler Fiorenza is concerned to make explicit and traceable links between her understanding of divine wisdom and the possibilities that a feminist understanding of the tradition offers.[25] She is concerned to make clear the relationship between the traditions of Christianity and the feminist articulated resource of divine wisdom. She draws attention in particular to the grammatical focus for wisdom as gendered form in both Hebrew (*Chokmah*) and Greek (*Sophia*) and she explores texts such as Proverbs 31 and Proverbs 9 to establish and build up a picture of the place and reference given to divine wisdom. Schüssler Fiorenza explains and justifies the authoritative and critical significance given to divine wisdom by a textual based characterization of the tradition. This establishes divine wisdom as participating in divine activity, as understood by the Christian tradition, in such a way as is consistent with and supportive of feminist values and concerns:

> She is the glory of G*d (Wisd. 7:25–26), and mediator of creation (Wisd. 8:5–6) and shares the throne of G*d (Wisd. 7:25–26). She rules over kings and is herself all powerful. She makes everything, renews everything, and permeates the cosmos (Wisd. 7:23, 27; 8:1, 5). "She is but one, yet can do everything, she makes all things new" (Wisd. 7:27). She is "intelligent and holy, free moving, clear, loving what is good, eager, beneficent, unique in her Way" (Wisd. 7:22). She is a people-loving spirit (Wisd. 1:6) who shares in the throne of G*d and in the ruling power of G*d (Wisd. 9:10). She is an initiate into the knowledge of G*d, collaborator in G*d's work, the brightness that streams from everlasting light, a pure effervescence of divine glory, and the image of G*d's goodness. In short, Divine Wisdom lives symbiotically with G*d (Wisd. 8:3f; 7:26). Kinship with Wisdom brings immortality and friendship with her, resulting in pure delight (Wisd. 10:17).[26]

From identified biblical evidence for a feminist critical recovery and engagement of divine wisdom, Schüssler Fiorenza and other feminist theologians offer the reconstructed tradition as a tool of justice. In this way the tradition is articulated as a key Christian resource for addressing situations of injustice. For example, Mary E. Hunt in 'Sophia's Sisters in Struggle: Kyriarchal Backlash, Feminist Vision' comments: 'In the beginning, Sophia struggled. The struggle continues, as feminists inspired by her Wisdom seek to bring about religiously informed justices in society at large and in Christian churches in particular.'[27]

It is specifically the qualities of divine wisdom as perceived by Christian feminist theologians that make the tradition such an important resource. These qualities include divine wisdom as powerful, creative, loving and justice-seeking. Maria Pilar Aquino's vision expresses this understanding clearly:

> The presence of Divine Wisdom, because it excludes oppressive and dehumanizing relationships, fosters and supports a world in which life is

worth living. Divine Wisdom sees the spiritualities, actions and attitudes of the kyriarchal elites as deserving of condemnation for dominating and exploiting humankind and the environment. So, for critical Wisdom, justice is the foundation of understanding, discernment, and the practice of an ethical way of life that can be considered right, honest, reasonable, and just. In these traditions, Divine Wisdom not only deliberately appears within social groups suffering under and resisting injustices but also empowers them to struggle against these injustices for liberation and its objectives.[28]

Conclusion

Divine wisdom is an increasingly prominent discourse of Christian feminist theology. The wisdom traditions are being recovered from the Jewish and Christian sources in a feminist creative process of reconstruction and used as a tool to address and transform contemporary situations of injustice. The viability of divine wisdom as such a tool of justice is linked to its roots in the traditions of Christianity, and particularly in terms of its links with biblical texts. These traceable roots, combined with a correlation between the characteristics of divine wisdom and the concerns, values and approaches of feminism, have led Christian feminist theologians to articulate a vision of divine wisdom as a powerful and relevant justice-based, transformative element of Christianity.

Notes

1. E. Cady Stanton, *The Woman's Bible* (US: Prometheus Books, 1999), p. 7.
2. E. Schüssler Fiorenza, 'Introduction: Walking in the Way of Wisdom', in M. P. Aquino and E. Schüssler Fiorenza (eds.), *In the Power of Wisdom: Feminist Spiritualities of Struggle* (London: SCM Press, 2000), p. 7.
3. S. Schroer, 'The Justice of Sophia: Biblical Wisdom Traditions and Feminist Discourses', in E. Schüssler Fiorenza (ed.), *Searching the Scriptures: Volume Two: A Feminist Commentary* (London: SCM Press, 1994), p. 17.
4. Ibid., p. 31.
5. W. J. Abraham, *Canon and Criterion in Christian Theology: From the Fathers to Feminism* (Oxford: Clarendon Press, 1998), pp. 433–4.
6. Ibid., pp. 464–5.
7. Schüssler Fiorenza, 'Walking in the Way of Wisdom', p. 7.
8. E. Schüssler Fiorenza, *In Memory of Her: A Feminist Theological Reconstruction of Christian Origins* (New York: Crossroad, 1983), p. xix.
9. Ibid., p. 28.
10. Ibid., p. 69.
11. V. Saiving, 'The human situation: a feminine view', *Journal of Religion*, 40 (1960), pp. 100–12. Reprinted in H. MacKinnon and M. McIntyre (eds.), *Readings in Ecology and Feminist Theology* (Kansas City: Sheed and Ward, 1980).
12. U. King, *Women and Spirituality: Voices of Protest and Promise*, 2nd edn. (Basingstoke: Macmillan Press, 1993), p. 158; G. M. Jantzen, *Becoming Divine: Towards a Feminist Philosophy of Religion* (Manchester: Manchester University Press, 1998), p. 159.
13. D. Hampson, *Theology and Feminism* (Oxford: Basil Blackwell, 1990), p. 122.
14. V. Saiving, 'The human situation: a feminine view', *Readings in Ecology*,

p. 3.
15. Ibid., p. 9.
16. Ibid., p. 12.
17. Ibid.
18. C. P. Christ and J. Plaskow (eds.), *Womanspirit Rising: A Feminist Reader in Religion* (San Francisco: Harper SanFrancisco, 1992), p. 29.
19. Schüssler Fiorenza, *In Memory of Her*, p. 41.
20. Ibid., pp. 69–70.
21. E. Schüssler Fiorenza, *Jesus: Miriam's Child, Sophia's Prophet: Critical Issues in Feminist Christology* (London: SCM Press, 1995), p. 133.
22. Ibid., p. 139.
23. Ibid., p. 132.
24. Ibid., p. 3.
25. Ibid., p. 133.
26. Ibid., pp. 135–6.
27. M. E. Hunt, 'Sophia's Sisters in Struggle: Kyriarchal Backlash, Feminist Vision', in Aquino and Schüssler Fiorenza (eds.), *In the Power of Wisdom*, p. 23.
28. M. P. Aquino, 'Towards a New World in the Power of Wisdom', in Aquino and Schüssler Fiorenza (eds.), *In the Power of Wisdom*, p. 132.

Taking the Emperor's Clothes Seriously:
The New Testament and the Roman Emperor[1]

Justin Meggitt

The figure of the Roman emperor has, until relatively recently, been of marginal interest to students of the New Testament. Even though interest has increased, it has not been the object of an extensive study since Stauffer's *Christ and the Caesars* in 1955[2] and has only played a significant part in a handful of other published works.[3] Indeed, those who have argued that the figure of the emperor is a sustained concern of any part of the New Testament have often found themselves the object of ridicule and their interest regarded as, at best, somewhat eccentric (an example of this can be seen in R. P. Martin's remarks about Karl Bornhäuser's *Jesus imperator mundi* in the former's *Carmen Christi*).[4] At first sight this general lack of concern about emperors is unsurprising. After all, the New Testament itself only directly refers to emperors in a few places, even if they do seem to cast a long shadow over some of its proceedings, albeit from the wings, as in Acts (where, in the final chapters, Nero appears to be something like Godot, often talked about but never putting in an appearance).[5] New Testament scholars are perhaps familiar with the fact that the term *euangellion* is also found in imperial propaganda at the time of the birth of Jesus or that Revelation 13 probably includes allusions to Nero and other emperors, but little beyond that.[6]

However, such a neglect of the figure of the Roman emperor is, I contend, a significant failing on the part of New Testament scholarship. *The Roman emperor was a central feature of the cultural context of the first century and must be taken consistently into account in exegesis of the New Testament.*[7]

Such a statement obviously requires justification. To do this I will need to begin by demonstrating the importance of the emperor in the lives of the inhabitants of the first-century empire. This is best achieved by examining the *content* of imperial ideology during this period,[8] and the *reception* of this ideology. It is useful to distinguish between its *public* reception (by which I mean the degree to which it contributed to the shared culture of the day) and its *private* reception (by which I mean its reception in non-public cultures, such as that of the individual, or the household or workplace).[9] Only when this is achieved can we turn back to the New Testament and demonstrate the validity of my opening claim.

Imperial Ideology

The imperial cult, the worship of the emperors, is one of the central elements in the ideology of the emperor and is a good place to start (though it is not, as is so often the case, the place to end).[10] After all, it is, as we shall see, through the images and symbols of the cult that the emperor was most regularly encountered by those he ruled. And it was in the cult that the ideology was at its most apparent and naked (often literally, as any cursory examination of its iconography will reveal).

The character of the imperial cult, at least in the eastern empire, is the subject of considerable debate at present, as can be seen by a cursory examination of the two most significant works on the subject: S. R. F. Price's *Rituals and Power: The Roman Imperial Cult in Asia Minor*[11] and Steven Friesen's *Twice Neokoros: Ephesus, Asia and the Cult of the Flavian Imperial Family*.[12] However, in crude terms we can say that the cult, although varying significantly in its form over time, and from location to location, claimed that the emperors, as rulers and benefactors of the world, were worthy of worship. This is illustrated by a quotation from Nicolaus of Damascus which describes the cult during the reign of Augustus:

> Because mankind addresses him thus (Sebastos)[13] in accordance with their estimation of his honour, they revere him with temples and sacrifices over islands and continents, organised by cities and provinces, matching the greatness of his virtue and repaying his benefactions towards them.[14]

Such opinions can also be found in a myriad of other literary sources, such as Horace, Seneca, Suetonius, Paterculus, and Virgil,[15] and formed the substance of numerous official inscriptions from the New Testament period.[16] For example, a famous inscription from Priene reads:

> ... the providence which divinely ordered our lives created with zeal and

munificence the most perfect good for our lives, by producing Augustus and filling him with virtue for the benefaction of humanity, sending us and those after us a saviour who put an end to war and established all things; ... when he appeared he exceeded the hopes of all those who anticipated good news (*euangellion*) not only by surpassing the benefactors born before him, but not even leaving those to come any hope of surpassing him: ... the birthday of the god marked for the world the beginning of the gospel (*euangellion*) of his coming.[17]

Another inscription from Cos reads: '(The) Emperor Caesar, son of god, god Sebastos has by his benefactions to all men outdone even the Olympian gods.'[18]

The *Res Gestae* of Augustus, the self-penned, public record of the achievements of that paradigmatic emperor opens in a similar vein: 'The achievements of the Divine Augustus, by which he brought the whole world under the empire of the Roman people ... '[19] Such an idea can also be observed expressed in other media. The temples of the cult itself (such as the Ara Pacis in Rome)[20] and various works of monumental and fine art, from bold triumphal arches and statues to the exquisite Gemma Augustea,[21] visually articulated this 'theology'. Nor should we overlook the coins of the period which, through their inscriptions and designs, expressed the same central message (a fact which is familiar to New Testament scholars from study of the 'Render Unto Caesar' pericope).[22] The basic ideas of the cult are easily accessible in a vast array of written and material remains from the New Testament world.

The Reception of the Imperial Cult

The picture of the emperor presented by authors of the period was well known and appears to have met with widespread approval. Although the specific levels of literacy in the Roman empire are difficult to determine, there is considerable evidence that this is the case.[23] The example of Virgil is particularly telling. Graffiti from Pompeii indicates that his readership went well beyond his own class,[24] and we are told (presumably plausibly) that some of his lines concerning the divinity of Augustus were rapturously received by a rowdy mob at an imperial games during his lifetime.[25] Indeed, there is evidence that his particular conceptualization of the divinity of the emperor continued to be influential long after his death.[26]

Inscriptions referring to the divinity of the emperor (often inscribed on statue bases and altars) were also significant in shaping public opinion; they were prominent, numerous and widely distributed throughout the empire and its cities, with thirteen such inscriptions to Augustus alone in the main market of Roman Athens, and at least one to the same emperor in virtually every significant urban settlement in the eastern empire.[27] Indeed, the *Res Gestae* was a *public* text that was put up in a number of cities. Although the original was written for Rome, three copies are in existence today from Ancyra, Pisidian Apollonia, and Pisidian Antioch, and there were, no doubt, many more. It too may therefore have been relatively well known and influential, although it should be added that the frequency of the public display of the language of the cult does not necessarily indicate that it was a well known and active component in the world-view of inhabitants. We should not underestimate the capacity for public inscriptions to be unnoticed after their initial construction even by those that lived their lives surrounded by them (it is indicative of this that in the process of destroying Alexandrian Jewish prayer halls (39 CE), a mob of gentiles seeking to promote the worship of Caligula actually destroyed dedications to previous emperors).[28]

If we turn to the non-written elements of first-century culture, and particularly those encountered in the urban environments of the eastern empire, the importance of imperial ideology in the public culture of its day becomes all the more visible. In physical terms the cult had a pervasive presence, it was the most widely and uniformly distributed of all the cults of the empire (its unique provincial administration facilitated this). Its temples were, for example, prominently displayed in most sizeable settlements (and a number of smaller, rural ones)[29] and dominated the public space of the towns and cities in which they were found. We can see this, for example, in Caesarea Maritima where the temple to Augustus was built on a raised platform overlooking the harbour and much of the city. They were impressive central features of many urban landscapes, well within the sacred boundaries (*pomerium*) of such cities. Indeed, for a first-century audience, more attuned to the 'differential charge' locations within Greco-Roman cities could possess,[30] such temples would have appeared all the more impressive, occupying, as they did, crucial sites in their symbolic geography (in Athens, for example, the cult temple was constructed in the Acropolis, near the Parthenon, in the historic and religious heart of the city). Cult buildings were especially concentrated in Rome, a place which functioned (in one sense) like Versailles or the Paris of Napoleon, as the shop-window of the regime, advertising the benefits of the *pax romana* and encouraging inhabitants of the empire to be willing and compliant participants in its maintenance.[31] It contained a number of remarkable constructions such as Augustus's Mausoleum (an enormous building, some forty metres high, topped with a bronze colossus of Augustus), the beautiful and ornate Ara Pacis, and a giant sundial (an obelisk taken from Egypt, signifying the defeat of Antony and Cleopatra which began his rule) erected in such a way as to demonstrate the cosmological significance of Augustus's birth (its shadow bisected the Ara Pacis on his birthday).[32] Numerous triumphal arches and columns also littered the city's streets and special imperial shrines marked their intersections. The importance of cult buildings, both within and outside the capital, was given further amplification through the coins of the period, which often included depictions of these in their designs.[33]

Imperial statues, associated with such buildings or independent of them, also filled up the public space of many cities and made their presence felt. The widespread and quite unprecedented standardization of the figures must also have cumulatively functioned to enhance their impact.[34] Many of these were aesthetically impressive and a substantial proportion were fashioned from precious metals.[35] The fact that many were colossi would also have added to the power of the imperial image being depicted (there are many existing examples of this, such as the colossus of Titus erected in Ephesus). Throughout the empire, such statues regularly portrayed the emperor as a god who stood (literally) head and shoulders above all others.

But the physical remains of the cult only give us a partial clue to its importance for those who actually lived their lives surrounded by its manifestations. The buildings and statues were not static but dynamic in the consciousness of the inhabitants of the first-century world, they were places about which regular public rituals, processions, sacrifices, and feasts would be centred, in which all members of the community would often to some extent be involved.[36] They were regularly the focus of community activities which could, especially upon the death of an emperor or a commemorative day associated with one of his family, become quite intense, and were unmatched by festivities undertaken for the sake of any other deities.[37] Zanker does not exaggerate when he observes that the buildings of the cult were the stage set against which the inhabitants of the empire lived their lives.[38]

Indeed, the affective quality of the material forms of the cult was heightened by legislation that helped it acquire almost numinous associations. For example, a slave fleeing from the rule of a harsh master could claim asylum by laying hold of an imperial statue, as could others in need of protection,[39] and anyone damaging a statue of an emperor or treating it with disrespect (by, for example, urinating in its vicinity)[40] could face the death penalty. The terror this last law struck into the hearts of inhabitants of the empire is demonstrated by an incident in the Acts of Peter in which a shattered imperial statue, broken in the course of a vigorous exorcism undertaken by Peter, was miraculously healed in response to the pleas of a terrified Christian, fearful of the consequences of leaving it in pieces.[41]

It should also be noted that the public dominance of the cult did not just focus upon its physical presence in the cities. It was not just the physical but also the temporal space that was transformed by imperial ideology. From early in the rule of Augustus it was suggested by the governor of Asia that each year should begin on the emperor's birthday, and this suggestion was enthusiastically taken up by the province.[42] Indeed it had already become conventional in the empire to calculate the date with reference to the number of years the divine figure had reigned (for example, a contract for the lease of a cow in Egypt reads, 'The fifth year of the dominion of Caesar, son of God').[43] Regular festivals associated with the imperial household and of course, the renaming of two of the months after Julius Caesar and Augustus respectively, helped to place the imperial stamp firmly upon the experience of time for the inhabitants of the empire.

Nor should we neglect the way that the cult clearly achieved prominence by the *negative* way that it disrupted and displaced competing focuses of religious allegiance (a significant point made by Susan Alcock).[44] The imperial god was essentially a new one; its continuity with other hero cults and the worship of Roma has been exaggerated. As Millar remarks:

> There is nothing anywhere to suggest that the scale of the cult-acts for Hellenistic kings had ever approached that which immediately appears for Augustus. Few cults of deceased Hellenistic kings lingered on, and only a modest range of evidence attest cults or games or shrines for even the major Roman figures of the late Republic. The sudden outburst of the celebration of Octavian/Augustus was a new phenomenon.[45]

But it was also, importantly, a jealous one. With the arrival of the cult of the emperor other public cults of divinized (historical) men were curtailed,[46] and even more established deities could suffer from its intolerance. Nero, for example, destroyed the oracle of Apollo by blocking up the sacred fissure with corpses of its adherents[47] whilst Caligula, rather famously, attempted (albeit unsuccessfully) to usurp the place of the Jewish god by having an effigy of himself erected in the temple (and his enthusiastic supporters successfully put statues of him in those prayer houses of the Jews in Alexandria which were too robust to be destroyed).[48] Indeed, Caligula gives us one of the most striking examples of this supercessionism (and one of the most appalling acts of artistic vandalism in the ancient world): he had the most famous cult statues from Greece shipped to Rome, where their heads were removed to be replaced by models of his own.[49]

It seems therefore fair to conclude that the ideology of the imperial cult was an influential component in the public culture of empire.

Private Reception of the Cult

Although such information allows us to *begin* to see the prominent position that the imperial cult held in the cultural experience of the first century, it is not enough to prove this conclusively to be the case. If we wish to evaluate its significance with any accuracy we must also determine whether it was an active component not just of the public, shared culture of the empire, but also the unofficial and private cultures that existed within the cities. Did it have a definite role in how the great mass of individuals conceptualized their world?

At first sight this may seem a strange question to ask. The imperial cult is often regarded as a purely public phenomenon, and a superficial one at that. After all, it is argued, the Romans themselves did not appear to take it seriously (Vespasian's famous deathbed joke, "I think I am becoming a god"[50] seems to indicate as much): it could only be believed by those who were either insane, such as Caligula, who went so far as to sacrifice to himself daily and made his beloved horse a high priest of his cult,[51] or irredeemably barbarian and by implication, stupid, such as the Britons of Colchester who built an enormous temple to the Divine Claudius.[52] The cult has often been seen as little more than a gross form of flattery, motivated by the political ambitions of provincial elites, or the consequence of crude manipulation or megalomania on the part of emperors, the best of which, it is often remarked, were reticent about its development.[53] But such characterizations are misguided and one cannot help assuming that it is, at least to a large extent, a consequence of mistaken assumptions about the nature of authentic religious belief.[54] The remarks Badian made some time ago in connection with the study of the deification of Alexander the Great are apposite in this respect: 'Modern Jews and Christians, or modern rationalists, from their different points of view, have always found it difficult to believe that the ancient Greeks took their religion seriously since it seems so patently absurd.'[55] The same could equally be said of the Romans.

However, it appears that the cult was enthusiastically practised in private as well as public, although the material demonstrating this has generally been neglected in studies to date and much more work remains to be done in this area. We find, for example, plenty of evidence that representations of emperors found their way into domestic and workshop shrines,[56] and that private shrines were dedicated to emperors from the earliest years of the cult.[57] Indeed, as Pleket has shown, from Augustus onwards, the emperors were the focus of 'mysteries' that resembled the long-established mysteries of the Hellenistic world, and drew substantial numbers of adherents.[58] Libations were poured out to the *genii* of emperors at every feast,[59] the names of deified emperors were invoked to solemnize oaths,[60] they were understood to be capable of carrying out healings,[61] and of hearing and answering prayers.[62] The appearance of the man-god himself could provoke devotion from onlookers[63] and such behaviour was not limited to non-Romans as is often supposed.[64] The figure of the emperor was clearly one about which a variety of lively and sincere religious beliefs had grown, convictions that can hardly be dismissed as superficial. Indeed, this can be seen in an array of apparently inconsequential objects that can be easily overlooked. The unmistakable symbols of the divine Caesars – for example, representations of cornucopiae (signifying the presence of the Golden Age), Capricorn (the sign of the zodiac associated with Augustus's conception),[65] the star of Julius Caesar (the first of the divinized Caesars) – can be found adorning a multitude of domestic artefacts found throughout the Mediterranean, such as oil lamps,[66] roof tiles,[67] personal medallions,[68] signet rings,[69] and even the Roman equivalent of piggy banks.[70] Of course, workshops determined the designs that were available to consumers but such evidence does reveal the significant place of imperial ideology in popular culture. An individual choosing to purchase an oil lamp decorated with imperial motifs, as so many evidently did, rather than with the perennially popular images of chariot racing, gladiators or copulation, was, in some sense, actively buying into the ideology.

Imperial Ideology: Beyond the Cult

So much for the cult. Although it would be foolish to demarcate too rigidly cultic and other depictions of the emperor, as in some way all imperial ideology was pervaded by religious conceptualizations of the imperial figure, the emperor was more than the cult, and imperial ideology was embodied in other forms and practices, many of which still require extensive examination (for example, its significance in the ideological construction of gender in the empire, and particularly of the body, is only just becoming visible).[71] Such wider manifestations of the ideology have often been overlooked in the exegesis of the New Testament because scholars specializing in its study have remained primarily interested in specifically 'religious' phenomena, and, with noticeable, and largely modern exceptions, have examined these in isolation from their wider cultural environment. Whilst it is impossible to present a comprehensive picture of the presence of the cult in this chapter, nonetheless it is useful to sketch three areas in which its presence can be seen.

1. Leisure

One of the major 'means of the transmission and diffusion of imperial ideology'[72] was the construction, throughout the empire, of buildings associated with the pursuit of specifically Roman forms of leisure: public baths, circuses, amphitheatres, and Roman-style theatres – a phenomenon recognized as one of the defining features of Roman culture (both by the Romans themselves and by others). Such buildings became inseparably associated with the figure of the emperor, and advertised the fact in a number ways, some more subtle than others. The amphitheatres, in particular, often provided an arena for celebrating imperial rule, a site for imperial pomp (sometimes of an overtly religious character).[73] Such activities allowed 'the audience to participate, however marginally, in imperial grandeur', in buildings designed to 'awe the viewer with the power of the state and its august ruler, but simultaneously to allow him [sic] his "moment of glory": a share in the pride and prestige of imperial achievement'.[74] It is unsurprising that the games had such a prominent place in his *Res Gestae* (22–23). As Toner has ably demonstrated, the practice and discourse of leisure became a vehicle for the propagation of imperial ideology.[75]

2. Moral Discourse

Another major vehicle for imperial ideology was the moral discourse of the empire, which, from the time of Augustus onwards, became dominated by an intense conservatism, bordering on archaism, particularly evident in its concern with the Roman family. The major element in this innovation was the unusual legislation that Augustus initiated that, although aimed primarily at the elite, for the first time made 'the private life of virtually every Roman ... a matter of the state's concern and regulation',[76] with the state taking upon itself the unusual role of not only arbiter but also prosecutor for crimes of immorality, crimes in which it had previously had no interest. The active dissemination of certain images of the imperial family helped support this development.[77] The depictions of Augustus himself, as the model *pater familias*, and various imperial women, such as his wife Livia, sister Octavia, or niece Antonia Augusta, as ideal Roman matrons, were particularly central in this respect.[78] Personal morality was a concern to which emperors consistently returned and became a key means by which they justified their dominance, even if, in their personal lives, they rather famously failed to practise what they preached.

3. Socio-Economic Exchange

Imperial ideology was also embodied in the closely related models of socio-economic exchange which became particularly prominent with the arrival of the Caesars: euergetism and patronage.

Although the notion of the *eueregetes*, the civic benefactor, predated Rome in the east, with the coming of the empire euergetism became far more significant and centred on the person of the emperor. The destruction of the voting assemblies of the eastern cities, which came about as a consequence of their inclusion in the empire, effectively left competition in the practice of benefactions as the only means by which the civic elites could compete for power in their localities; and success in this was dependent upon attaining the patronage of the man who sat at the top of the social pyramid. The emperor became the patron *par excellence* (as we can see in the earlier quotation from Nicolaus of Damascus) and the model for (and patron of) the local benefactors outside Rome, who were in turn patrons of others lower down the socio-economic scale (he was, however, the only *euergetes* of Rome itself – no one else was allowed to make benefactions in that city).[79] Although patronage certainly was not the all-pervasive phenomenon so often assumed by classical and New Testament scholars,[80] and was functionally insignificant for most, it was a prominent component of imperial culture and a means by which the rule of the emperors was conceptualized and sustained.

Reception

Evidence for the generally positive public reception of the ideology of leisure is clear: the sheer proliferation of the facilities, and epigraphic and literary evidence of their heavy use in the first-century period indicates as much. It is obvious also, from the appearance of sporting and acting 'celebrities' in the empire, that this element of the imperial programme became a lively component in the private lives of inhabitants of the empire.[81] Likewise, the positive public and private reception of imperial moral discourse is also confirmed by, for example, the distinctive changes in group portraiture and the style of epitaphs that are a distinguishing feature of the early empire.[82] And the same, I believe, can be demonstrated from epigraphic and papyrological evidence of euergetism and patronage.[83]

But before we leave this analysis of imperial ideology and turn to the New Testament, I would like to make a few qualifying remarks. It should not be assumed that imperial ideology was always readily or simply accepted, either at the public or private level. Its manifestations were capable of being mocked and derided (we find, for example, the simple but telling word 'enough' scratched upon one of the numerous triumphal arches which adorned the capital during the reign of Domitian).[84] Some of its 'theological' claims could be hard for some to swallow.[85] The elements of the ideology could also be appropriated in ways that were clearly never intended by its proponents. For example, during Tiberius's rule, a woman followed the senator Gaius Cestius Gallus around Rome, hurling abuse at him whilst clutching a portrait of the emperor and thus avoiding prosecution, a practice that was far from uncommon.[86] Indeed, the figure of the emperor was not necessarily treated with respect by the general population (piss pots used by fullers in Rome were nicknamed *Vespasiani* after the emperor who introduced an unpopular tax upon them).[87] And of course, the content and form of the ideology could vary between emperors (though this should not be exaggerated; even Nero, whose departures from imperial conventions were as notorious as they were absurd, self-consciously modelled himself upon Augustus, for example, issuing coins depicting the Ara Pacis).[88]

The New Testament

In the light of the case we have presented for the significance of the figure of the emperor in the New Testament world, albeit with these final qualifications in mind, let us now turn back to the New Testament itself and examine a few of its implications.

1. Christology

In view of the central place of the emperor in the lives of the inhabitants of the empire, the figure of the Roman emperor must be given a far more significant place in any attempt to discern the nature of formative Christology than has hitherto been recognized. Indeed, its cultural significance warrants giving it a position in Christological discussion equal to that accorded to at least some of the material from the Jewish background in the analysis of the genesis and development of early Christian ideas about Jesus. If this appears a rather rash statement, it is perhaps worth recalling just how problematic some of these sources can be when questions about the dating, provenance or dissemination are asked: the *Similitudes of Enoch* (1 Enoch 37–71) which contains so many crucial references to Christological titles otherwise thin on the ground elsewhere outside the New Testament (most notably the enigmatic 'Son of Man'),[89] is first attested *only* in a fifteenth-century Ethiopic manuscript.[90] It will no longer do for New Testament scholars to place the Roman emperor amongst the ranks of divine men, gnostic redeemers, divinized heroes and other assorted and 'Hellenistic' characters and then dismiss his significance by reason of the disreputable company that he keeps. He is far too important for that to be the case. To put the matter simply: how many oil lamps or coins do we have from the first century featuring Apollonius of Tyana? How many games were held in his honour? How many temples were dedicated to him? How many tax statements were dated according to his birth? We must come to terms with the fact that the development of ideas about Christ could not have occurred independently of the influence of ideas about the Roman emperor. The alternative is to believe, in the light of the information we have just surveyed that, in the words of Deissmann, 'St Paul and his fellow believers went through the world blindfolded'.[91]

But it is one thing to say that ideas about the emperor and ideas about Christ are clearly related; it is another to say *how* they are related. It is hard to answer this without descending into unsatisfying, vague generalizations, and I apologize if what follows appears to have something of that quality about it. This is not the place to examine the nature of this relationship with any precision – although I think a more extended study is quite a feasible undertaking and may yield valuable results – rather I will make a few observations about the alternative characterizations of the relationship that have been suggested.

1) It is maintained by some that the relationship was essentially *analogical-sequential*: that is, imperial ideology did not directly shape ideas about Christ but, by virtue of the obvious analogies between some key elements of both, it made the ideas about Christ preached by the early Christians easily comprehensible and attractive to pagans. This is the position, for example, taken by Kreitzer. He suggests that somehow the apotheosis of the emperor provided a parallel to the Christian notion of incarnation (albeit in reverse), and one which made it all the more easy for Christianity to flourish amongst pagans to an extent which was impossible for Judaism, because the latter had a far less permeable barrier between the human and the divine realms.[92]

Although I cannot agree with the details of Kreitzer's argument, in general terms such a position is plausible, as far as it goes, but it does not go very far. A *sequential* understanding of the relationship assumes that individuals attracted to Christianity from non-Jewish backgrounds ceased to be influenced by pagan ideas, such as those drawn from the imperial cult – either positively or negatively – upon conversion. This seems rather problematic. The New Testament itself testifies to the persistence of pagan practices amongst the early communities and patterns of socialization by believers that brought them into contact with pagans on a regular basis (for example, 1 Corinthians 8 and 10). Such a *sequential* model, by itself, cannot describe the nature of the relationship that must have been far more dynamic than is implied by the use of such words as 'backdrop' or 'heritage', commonly used by proponents of this position to describe the place of the imperial cult in respect to the development of Christology.

2) It is also claimed that the relationship was one of *dependency* or that it was *genealogical* in its nature. I should emphasize that there is nothing methodologically wrong with this assertion, although it does go against the grain for many New Testament scholars, who, as J. Z. Smith has observed, are still dominated by the essentially apologetic (and Protestant) myth of Christian autochthony.[93] And, on a superficial level, this kind of relationship appears to be indicated by the profusion of terms which are associated with both the emperor and the figure of Christ in the New Testament,[94] such as *theos* (deus), *theou uios* (divi filius), *kurios* (dominus), *basileus* (imperator), *soter* (servator), *archiereus* (pontifex maximus), *euangellion* (evangellium), *parousia* (adventus), and others. However, I believe that this way of characterizing the relationship is also flawed.

Firstly, the philological parallels on closer examination appear rather less impressive. If we take the business of comparison seriously, we must place these terms back in their respective contexts, and then determine the meaning they have within these contexts, before looking again to see if the meanings they were intended to convey are significantly close to warrant a claim of dependency. The coincidence of terminology, however striking, is simply not enough.[95] For example, the expression 'Son of God' occurs in both the context of the imperial cult and in the New Testament but it implied radically different things in both: in the former it refers to an emperor who was, in some sense, a son of both a previously divinized emperor, and also, at the same time, of a particular god (for example, Apollo for Augustus);[96] an impressive god perhaps, but still one amongst many. Such a meaning appears quite alien to the sense of the expression anywhere in the New Testament. Of course, ultimately, the plausibility of any speculations in this regard depends upon the degree of correlation considered significant, and the degree of abstraction allowed in the analysis. But if the relationship were one of dependency we would expect more obvious resemblances than the evidence appears to give us.

Secondly, what I take to be the fundamental Christological datum, that which is generative of all subsequent Christological developments, the resurrection (Rom. 1.4, 10.9 etc.) has no parallel in imperial ideology whatsoever.[97] One would expect some acute resemblance here, if there were some genealogical link.

3) However, I believe that the relationship is neither analogical-sequential nor genealogical but can be best described as one of *polemical parallelism*. The earliest strata in the traditions indicate that ideas about Christ were recognized as usurping claims made about emperors, particularly in respect to his claims of kingship. This is especially visible in details of the passion narrative, such as the detail of Jesus's mocking[98] and the wording of the *titulus*,[99] but is also evident elsewhere. This characteristic of New Testament Christology is often overlooked by New Testament scholars who, despite the evidence from Jn. 19.15, Acts 17.7, 1 Tim. 2.2, and 1 Pet. 2.17, appear ignorant of the fact that although the Romans were adamant that they were not ruled by a king, their emperor was considered to be one by non-Romans and was popularly referred to as one (indeed, the reticence of Romans to recognize that they were ruled by a monarchy was bewildering to others).[100] The early Christians seem to have shaped their Christology, even when they were forging it out of distinctly 'unpagan' elements, with this in mind. For example, the so-called Christ hymn of Phil. 2.5–11, which may be one of the oldest pieces of Christological evidence we possess, culminates with a quotation from Isa. 45.23 ('every knee shall bow ... and every tongue confess'). These words, originally a reference to the universal rule of God, are applied to Jesus[101] but would have had undeniable resonances for anyone familiar with the articulation of imperial ideology (they have, for example, clear parallels to the language of the *Res Gestae*). The application of this text in Phil. 2.10–11 is effectively subversive of the claims of the emperors: it flatly contradicted one of the central claims made for them. Given the similarities between some of the major themes of the Philippians hymn and the chief characteristics of the emperor cult (the divine origin or pre-existence of the subject, his apotheosis by acclamation at death, his ubiquitous rule and receipt of universal homage) which have long been noted, and have received thorough attention,[102] it is likely that the original composer of these lines, whoever they were, intended to assert the superiority of Christ over Caesar. (The hymn was not *only* intended to be read in such a way though; it is fair to say, with Seeley, that 'no single background can accommodate the hymn'.)[103]

Polemical parallelism seems the most instructive way of characterizing the role of ideas about the Roman emperor in the development of

Christology.

2. Politics

A more thoroughgoing awareness of the nature of imperial ideology in the New Testament world should also lead us to think again about the political character of the early Christian communities. Too often discussion of the politics of the New Testament begins and ends with the examination of a handful of texts, such as Romans 13 and Revelation 13, which appear to be obviously pertinent to such a concern. Although some, such as Elliott[104] and Wengst,[105] have gone beyond this, and asked wider, ideological questions, the study of the relationship of early Christians to imperial ideology is still dogged by a failure to take the breadth of the encounter seriously. However, a knowledge of the extent of this ideology, and the areas of life it encompassed, will allow us to give a fuller treatment of the question. We can locate far more areas in which to discern whether the early Christians supported or critiqued the rule of Roman emperor.

A couple of examples will illustrate this:

1) Paul's advocacy of celibacy, politically innocuous to us, would have been rather less so to his contemporaries, given the character of imperial ideology. According to Cassius Dio, Augustus equated the 'unmarried life with the immoral way of life'.[106] As Fiorenza has observed, 'Paul's advice to remain free from the marriage bond was a frontal assault upon the institutions of existing law and the general cultural ethos, especially since it was given to a people who lived in the urban centres of the Roman Empire.'[107] In many ways it is even more true of the anti-family tradition which is so apparent elsewhere in the New Testament.[108]

2) Likewise, despite the claims of many New Testament scholars, the New Testament appears to be, generally, hostile to the phenomenon of patronage.[109] This is clearly expressed, for example, in Lk. 22.25, where the disciples are told not to be like the *euergetai* of the gentiles[110] but is also implied in the various traditions within the New Testament which call for a mutual ethic amongst the believers which undermines the need for patronage.[111] It is also subverted in various ways in the New Testament: Paul, for example, plays with its emotive language and conventions in a striking way (as in Rom. 16.1–2 where he rather strangely writes a letter of recommendation *on behalf of* his patron Phoebe, a shocking and rather bizarre departure from convention). It is perhaps unsurprising that the

New Testament contains such material as patronage was essentially exploitative for the person in the inferior position in the relationship. But such responses must not be understood as motivated by solely economic concerns. They must be interpreted, in part, in the light of imperial ideology, as, for example, Kraybill has argued in his reading of Revelation.[112]

3. Gender Relations

The situation of women in early Christianity has always been something of an enigma. Regardless of how such notorious verses as 1 Cor. 11.2–16, 1 Cor. 14.34, or 1 Tim. 2.12 are interpreted, it is evident that, at the earliest stages at least, women such as Phoebe, Junia, Lydia, and Priscilla held positions of authority amongst the men and women who constituted the nascent communities. Pagan criticism of Christianity corroborates this striking feature.[113] The explanation for this is hard to arrive at. However, it will not do to contrast supposedly paradigmatic, enlightened verses from the New Testament – such as Gal. 3.28 – with rather less endearing texts culled from a narrow range of pagan and Jewish sources, and maintain that one has uncovered the causal factor: the essential character of the new religion. Such an argument is arbitrary and decontextual. Other factors clearly played a part in this development, not least the unrelated growth, during this period, in the numbers of independent women who had the freedom to join a new cult such as Christianity. The explanation for this phenomenon is likewise difficult to ascertain. Changes in legal convention (the increasing dominance of non-*manus* marriage), and the increasing influence of regional traditions[114] go some way to providing an answer but the prominence given to women from the imperial family in imperial ideology is also significant: it allowed greater cultural space for some women to achieve greater autonomy and authority than had previously been the case.

Conclusions

This has been a very cursory survey of a vast subject, and the conclusions I have drawn, I concede, are rather provisional, and perhaps contentious. But I hope that my analysis will at least have brought the emperor back into focus and demonstrated the value of doing this for those who wish to scrutinize the New Testament in its context. There is much to be gained by giving due attention to this figure, particularly when awareness is shown of its ideological character and careful attention is paid to the question of its reception. Indeed, exegetes of the New Testament have much to lose if they do not do so.

Notes

1. A version of this paper was originally delivered at a number of research seminars in Oxford and Cambridge in 1997, including one at Westminster College where, for a couple of years, I was privileged to be able to work alongside Philip Budd in teaching Biblical and Hermeneutical Studies. It would not have been written without Philip's generous encouragement and interest.

   In more recent years a number of significant studies have appeared, most notably: A. Brent, *The Imperial Cult and the Development of Church Order. Concepts and Images of Authority in Paganism and Early Christianity Before the Age of Cyprian* (Leiden: Brill, 1999); W. Carter, *Matthew and Empire. Initial Explorations* (Harrisburg: Trinity Press International, 2001); S. J. Friesen, *Imperial Cults and the Apocalypse of John. Reading Revelation in the Ruins* (Oxford: Oxford University Press, 2001); P. Oakes, *Philippians. From People to Letter* (Cambridge: Cambridge University Press, 2001); and I. Gradel, *Emperor Worship and Roman Religion* (Oxford: Clarendon Press, 2002).

2. E. Stauffer, *Christ and the Caesars: Historical Sketches* (London: SCM, 1955).

3. See, for example, K. Wengst, *Pax Romana and the Peace of Jesus Christ* (London: SCM, 1987).

4. Martin quotes Henry's estimate of Bornhäuser approvingly: '... imagination can hardly go to more extreme limits than in his theory'. R. P. Martin, *Carmen Christi: Philippians 2:5–11 in Recent Interpretation and in the Setting of Early Christian Worship* (Grand Rapids: Eerdmans, 1983), p. 81; K. Bornhäuser, *Jesus imperator mundi* (Gütersloh: C. Bertelsmann, 1938).

5. Lk. 2.1 (Augustus); 3.1 (Tiberius); Acts 11.28, 18.2 (Claudius). More general references are found in Mt. 22.15–22, Mk. 12.13–17, Lk. 20.20–26; Jn. 19.12–15; Phil. 4.22; 1 Pet. 2.13, 17.

6. Rev. 13.3, 14, 18.

7. By culture I mean 'a system of shared meaning and value, and the symbolic forms (performances, artefacts) in which they are expressed or embodied'. P. Burke, *Popular Culture in Early Modern Europe* (London: Temple Smith, 1978), p. xi.

8. Given the debates that rage around the term 'ideology' I had better clarify what I mean by the expression 'imperial ideology': it is the cluster of interrelated, mutually suggestive ideas, practices, and their material forms, that articulated and legitimized the dominance of the Roman emperor in the Roman world.

9. There were a variety of ways that 'public' and 'private' could be conceptualized in the empire and we should be careful not to assume too close a resemblance with contemporary understandings. See, for example, Vitruvius, *On Architecture* 6.5. See also P. Veyne, 'The Roman Empire' in P. Veyne (ed.), *A History of Private Life* (Cambridge, MA: Belknap Press, 1987), pp. 205–34.

10. Though I do not mean by this to underestimate the religious nature of the cult, which some are prone to do. See, for example, A. Kee, 'The Imperial Cult: The Unmasking of an Ideology', *Scottish Journal of Religious Studies*, 6 (1985), pp. 112–28.

11. S. R. F. Price, *Rituals and Power: The Roman Imperial Cult in Asia Minor* (Cambridge: Cambridge University Press, 1984).

12. S. J. Friesen, *Twice Neokoros: Ephesus, Asia and the Cult of the Flavian Imperial Family* (Leiden: Brill, 1993).

13. Or 'Augustus' – worthy of reverence/worship.

14. F. Jacoby, *Die Fragmente der griechischen Historiker* (Leiden: Brill, 1923–1958), 90 F 125.

15. Horace, *Odes* 1.12.49; Seneca, *De Clementia* 1.1.2; Suetonius, *Augustus* 94; Velleius Paterculus, *History of Rome* 2.126.2–5, Virgil, *Aeneid* 6.789–794.

16. A. Benjamin and A. Raubitschek, 'Arae Augusti', *Hesperia*, 28 (1959), pp. 65–85.

17. Adapted from Price, *Rituals and Power*, p. 54.

18. Price, *Rituals and Power*, p. 55.

19. See P. A. Brunt and J. M. Moore, *Res Gestae Divi Augusti: The Achievements of the Divine Augustus* (Oxford: Oxford University Press, 1967), pp. 18–19.

20. On the Ara Pacis see N. Hannestad, *Roman Art and Imperial Policy* (Aarhus: Aarhus University Press, 1986), pp. 62–74; J. Elsner, 'Cult

and Sculpture: Sacrifice in the Ara Pacis Augustae', *Journal of Roman Studies*, 81 (1991), pp. 50–61; D. Castriota, *The Ara Pacis Augustae and the Imagery of Abundance in Later Greek and Early Roman Imperial Art* (Princeton: Princeton University Press, 1995).

21. See P. Zanker, *The Power of Images in the Age of Augustus* (Ann Arbor: The University of Michigan Press, 1990), pp. 230–3 and Hannestad, *Roman Art*, pp. 78–82. Augustus is depicted as Jupiter, the universal ruler, being crowned by Oikoumene, the personification of the inhabited world.

22. The coin which is crucial to this pericope was probably a denarius of Tiberius. It is likely to have been one from an issue in which, on the obverse, Tiberius is shown in full Olympian nakedness, adorned with a laurel wreath (a sign of divinity) and is described as 'Emperor Tiberius, August Son of the August God'. On the reverse Tiberius's mother is depicted in another Olympian pose, with a sceptre and olive branch. Above her are the words (referring to Tiberius) 'Pontifex Maximus'. As Stauffer rightly remarks, 'The coin, in brief, is a symbol of both power and of the cult' (*Christ and the Caesars*, p. 125). See also H. Hart, 'The Coin of "Render unto Caesar": A Note on Some Aspects of Mark 12:13–17; Matt. 22:15–22; Luke 20:20–26', in E. Bammel and C. F. D. Moule (eds.), *Jesus and the Politics of His Day* (Cambridge: Cambridge University Press, 1984), pp. 241–8.

23. See A. K. Bowman, 'Literacy in the Roman Empire: Mass and Mode', in J. Humphrey (ed.), *Literacy in the Roman World* (Ann Arbor: Journal of Roman Archaeology, 1991), pp. 119–31. Evidence for participation in literate culture can be seen in such details as Nero's use of placards to advertise his 'triumph' following his tour of Greece (Cassius Dio 62.20).

24. H. H. Tanzer, *The Common People of Pompeii. A Study of the Graffiti* (Baltimore: Johns Hopkins University Press, 1939), pp. 83–84. The remarkable popularity of Virgil may be indicated by the fragments of the *Aeneid* found in letters as far apart as Vindolanda (*Tab. Vindol.* II. 118) and Masada (*Doc. Masada.* 721).

25. Tacitus, *Dialogue* 13.

26. Scriptores Historiae Augustae, *Albinus* 5.2.

27. Benjamin and Raubitschek, 'Arae Augusti'.

28. Philo, *Embassy to Gaius* 133.

29. See, for example, the catalogue of imperial temples and shrines in Asia Minor in Price, *Rituals and Power*, pp. 249–64.

30. See R. Laurence, *Roman Pompeii: Space and Society* (London: Routledge, 1994) and A. Wallace-Hadrill, 'Public Honour and Private Shame: The Urban Texture of Pompeii', in J. Cornell and K. Lomas (eds.), *Urban Society in Roman Italy* (London: UCL Press, 1995), pp. 39–62.

31. P. Veyne, *Bread and Circuses: Historical Sociology and Political Pluralism* (Harmondsworth: Penguin, 1992), p. 385. Rome was not, of course, the only showpiece city. See, for example, the remarks of Tiridates (King of Armenia) about the cities of Asia (Cassius Dio 63.7).

32. Zanker, *The Power of Images*, pp. 144–5.

33. See T. L. Donaldson, *Ancient Architecture on Greek and Roman Coins and Medals* (Chicago: Argonaut, 1965).

34. Zanker, *The Power of Images*, p. 301.

35. See Suetonius, *Caligula* 22; Cassius Dio 67.8.1. See K. Scott, 'The Significance of Statues in Precious Metals in Emperor Worship', *Transactions and Proceedings of the American Philological Association*, 62 (1931), pp. 101–23.

36. Philo, *Embassy to Gaius* 280.

37. Zanker, *The Power of Images*, p. 114. For the funeral of Augustus see Cassius Dio 56.34, 42–47.

38. Zanker, *The Power of Images*, p. 299.

39. Cassius Dio 47.19.2; Tacitus, *Annals* 3.36; cf. also Suetonius, *Augustus* 17.5; Seneca, *De Clementia* 1.18.2. For statues of living emperors affording protection see Tacitus, *Annals* 3.63; Suetonius, *Tiberius* 58. See K. R. Bradley, *Slaves and Masters in the Roman Empire: A Study in Social Control* (Oxford: Oxford University Press, 1987), pp. 124–5.

40. Scriptores Historiae Augustae, *Caracalla* 5.7.

41. Acts of Peter 11. See Justinian, *Digest* 48.4.4–6. Cf. also Cassius Dio 62.23.

42. Price, *Rituals and Power*, p. 61.

43. J. R. Rea, 'Lease of a Red Cow Called Thayris', *Journal of Egyptian Archaeology*, 68 (1982), pp. 272–82. Cf. Lk. 3.1.

44. S. E. Alcock, 'Archaeology and Imperialism: Roman Expansion and the Greek City', *Journal of Mediterranean Archaeology*, 2 (1989), p. 123.

45. F. Millar, 'The Impact of Monarchy' in F. Millar and E. Segal (eds.),

Caesar Augustus: Seven Aspects (Oxford: Clarendon Press, 1984), p. 53.

46. Price, *Rituals and Power*, p. 49.

47. Cassius Dio 62.14.

48. Josephus, *Antiquities* 18.257–305; Philo, *Embassy to Gaius* 134.

49. Cassius Dio 59.28; Suetonius, *Caligula* 22. Such claims made sense within the conceptual world of paganism in which, for a god, 'the height of prestige was to dominate the others: there was no true sovereignty except in relation to other deities'. R. Turcan, *The Cults of the Roman Empire* (Oxford: Blackwell, 1996), p. 331.

50. Suetonius, *Vespasian* 23. See also Cassius Dio 59.26 for the scepticism of a provincial shoemaker.

51. Cassius Dio 59.28. For an attempt to understand Caligula's psychology in this respect, see C. J. Simpson, 'Caligula's cult: immolation, immortality, intent', in A. Small (ed.), *Subject and Ruler: The Cult of the Ruling Power in Classical Antiquity* (Ann Arbor: Journal of Roman Achaeology, 1996), pp. 63–72.

52. As a god hostile to Claudius's admission to the ranks of the deities remarks in Seneca's *Apocolocyntosis* 8.3: 'Is it not enough that he has a temple in Britain, that savages now worship him, as if he were a god ...'

53. Suetonius, *Augustus* 52. See also Claudius's response to the Alexandrians in E. M. Smallwood, *Documents Illustrating the Principates of Gaius, Claudius and Nero* (Cambridge: Cambridge University Press, 1967), no. 370.11.48.

54. See, for example, Price, *Rituals and Power*, pp. 15–22.

55. E. Badian, 'The Deification of Alexander the Great', in H. J. Bell (ed.), *Ancient Macedonian Studies in Honour of Charles F. Edson* (Thessaloniki: Institute for Balkan Studies, 1981), p. 31.

56. J. M. Santero, 'The Cultores Augustii and the Private Worship of the Roman Emperor', *Athenaeum (Pavia)*, 61 (1983), pp. 111–25. For the former see also Zanker, *The Power of Images*, p. 266 and the latter, T. Bakker, *Living and Working with the Gods: Studies of Evidence for Private Religion and its Material Environment in the City of Ostia (100-500 AD)* (Amsterdam: J. C. Gieben, 1994), p. 207. For evidence of the popularity of imperial images, of even the cheapest and poorest kinds, see Fronto, *To Marcus as Caesar* 4.12.4. Horace, writing in the lifetime of Augustus, describes an Italian peasant placing an image

of the emperor with his household gods (*Odes* 4.5.31–32) as did Ovid (*Ex Ponto* 2.8.1 and 4.9.105–106). Such private images were evidently popular as we can tell from their presence in wills (Santero, 'The Cultores Augustii', p. 115). Emperors were also keen to include representations of other emperors in their *lararia*. See, for example, Scriptores Historiae Augustae, *Alexander Severus* 29.2; 31.4–5.

57. See, for example, the altar consecrated to Augustus by Vicanus in Salacia in Spain in 10 CE (*Corpus Inscriptionum Latinum* II. 5182).

58. H. W. Pleket, 'An Aspect of the Emperor Cult: Imperial Mysteries', *Harvard Theological Review*, 58 (1965), pp. 331–47. Augustus' mysteries were still celebrated 150 years after his death.

59. Cassius Dio 51.19.7; Zanker, *The Power of Images*, p. 304.

60. For example, *Inscriptiones Latinae Selectae* 190 (37 CE).

61. Suetonius, *Vespasian* 7. For the most comprehensive survey of this aspect of the emperor's image see G. Ziethen, 'Heilung und römischer Kaiserkult', *Sudhoffs Archiv*, 78 (1994), pp. 171–91.

62. For example, Suetonius, *Julius* 85; Virgil, *Eclogue* 9.46–49; Valerius, *Maximus* 1.6.13; Virgil, *Georgics* 1.24–46; Virgil, *Aeneid* 1.286-90; Ovid, *Ex Ponto* 4.9.127; 4.13.24. See D. Fishwick, 'Seneca and the Temple of Divus Claudius', *Britannia*, 22 (1991), p. 140.

63. Suetonius, *Augustus* 98. See also Velleius Paterculus, *History of Rome* 2.107.

64. Virgil, *Eclogue* 1.6–8; Zanker, *The Power of Images*, p. 236.

65. See T. Barton, 'Augustus and Capricorn: Astrological Polyvalence and Imperial Ritual', *Journal of Roman Studies*, 85 (1995), pp. 33–51.

66. Zanker, *The Power of Images*, p. 274.

67. Zanker, *The Power of Images*, p. 84.

68. See P. Veyne, 'Tenir un Buste', *Cahiers de Byra*, 8 (1958), pp. 61–85.

69. Zanker, *The Power of Images*, p. 84.

70. Zanker, *The Power of Images*, p. 275.

71. See, for example, B. Kellum, 'The Phallus as Signifier: The Forum of Augustus and the Rituals of Masculinity', in N. Kampen (ed.), *Sexuality in Ancient Art: The Near East, Egypt, Greece and Italy* (Cambridge: Cambridge University Press, 1996), pp. 170–83.

72. R. Beacham, *The Roman Theatre and Its Audience* (London: Routledge, 1991), p. 163.

73. See J. A. Hanson, *Roman Theatre Temples* (Princeton: Princeton University Press, 1959). The religious nature of the games was

explicit (see, for example, from very different perspectives, Martial, *On the Spectacles* and Tertullian, *On the Spectacles*) and often rather gruesome (see K. M. Coleman, 'Roman Executions Staged as Mythological Enactments', *Journal of Roman Studies*, 80 (1990), pp. 44–73). The emperor often initiated and presided over such entertainments.

74. Beacham, *The Roman Theatre*, p. 189.

75. J. P. Toner, *Leisure and Ancient Rome* (Cambridge: Polity, 1995).

76. K. Galinsky, *Augustan Culture: An Intrepretative Introduction* (Princeton: Princeton University Press, 1996), p. 128. See, in particular, *Lex Julia de maritandis ordinibus* (18 BCE) and *Lex Papia Poppaea* (9 CE).

77. For example, the reliefs featuring the imperial family found on the Ara Pacis. However, not all attempts at presenting such an image were successful (Suetonius, *Augustus* 34.1).

78. Cults to these women are also found in the empire although some of the evidence is rather less obvious than it might at first appear. See M. Hoskins-Walbank, 'Pausaunias, Octavia and Temple E at Corinth', *British School at Athens*, 84 (1989), pp. 361–94.

79. Veyne, *Bread and Circuses*, pp. 386–390.

80. J. J. Meggitt, *Paul, Poverty and Survival* (Edinburgh: T & T Clark, 1998), pp. 168–70.

81. Toner, *Leisure and Ancient Rome*, p. 78.

82. See D. E. Kleiner, *Roman Group Portraiture: The Funerary Reliefs of the Late Republic and Early Empire* (London: Garland, 1977); Zanker, *The Power of Images*, p. 292.

83. For example, *Corpus Inscriptionum Latinum* VI, 21975.

84. Suetonius, *Domitian* 13.

85. For example, those surrounding an emperor's miraculous birth. See Philostratus, *Life of Apollonius of Tyana* 7.24.

86. Tacitus, *Annals* 3.36.

87. Martial, *Epigrams* 6.93; Suetonius, *Vespasian* 23.3; Cassius Dio 65.14.

88. Suetonius, *Nero* 10.1. In many ways the cult was polymorphous with emperors defining the parameters.

89. See G. W. E. Nicklesburg, 'Salvation without and with a Messiah: Developing Beliefs in Writings Ascribed to Enoch', in J. Neusner, W. S. Green and E. S. Frerichs (eds.), *Judaisms and Their Messiahs* (Cambridge: Cambridge University Press, 1987), pp. 49–68.

90. M. A. Knibb, '1 Enoch', in H. F. D. Sparks (ed.), *The Apocryphal Old*

Testament (Oxford: Clarendon Press, 1985), p. 174.

91. A. Deissmann, *Light from the Ancient East*, 2nd ed. (London: Hodder and Stoughton, 1910), p. 344.

92. L. Kreitzer, *Striking New Images. Roman Imperial Coinage and the New Testament World* (Sheffield: Sheffield Academic Press, 1996), p. 98.

93. J. Z. Smith, *Drudgery Divine: On the Comparison of Early Christianities and the Religions of Late Antiquity* (London: SOAS, 1990), pp. 45–6.

94. See Deissmann, *Light*, pp. 347–400 for examples of all the following parallels (and more): god, son of god, lord, king (emperor), saviour, high priest, good news, (second) coming.

95. It is customary to refer at this point to the influential article by Samuel Sandmel ('Parallelomania', *Journal of Biblical Literature*, 81 (1962), pp. 3–13) although the point is well made in other more recent works, such as D. Hall, *Seven Pillories of Wisdom* (Macon: Mercer University Press, 1990) and D. A. Carson, *Exegetical Fallacies* (Carlisle: Paternoster, 1996).

96. Suetonius, *Augustus* 94.

97. The traditions of Nero's return bear no resemblance to this (see Tacitus, *Histories* 2.9, John of Antioch, fr. 104; Suetonius, *Nero* 57.2; Dio Chrysostom, *Orations* 21.10; Sibylline Oracles 8.157). For a discussion of these traditions see R. Bauckham, *The Climax of Prophecy* (Edinburgh: T & T Clark, 1993), pp. 384–452.

98. Mt. 27.27–31; Mk. 15.16–20; Jn. 19.1–3.

99. Mt. 27.37, Mk. 15.26, Lk. 23.38, Jn. 19.19, 21.

100. Cassius Dio 53.17.

101. Though cf. Rom. 14.11.

102. D. Seeley, 'The Background of the Philippians Hymn (2:6–11)', *Journal of Higher Criticism*, 1 (1994), pp. 49–74.

103. Seeley, 'Background', p. 51.

104. N. Elliott, *Liberating Paul. The Justice of God and the Politics of the Apostle* (Sheffield: Sheffield Academic Press, 1995).

105. Wengst, *Pax Romana*.

106. Cassius Dio 56.6.6–7.2.

107. E. S. Fiorenza, *In Memory of Her: A Feminist Reconstruction of Christian Origins* (London: SCM, 1983), p. 225. This suggestion is also extensively discussed by E. Pagels in 'Christian Apologists and the "The Fall of the Angels": An Attack on Roman Imperial Power', *Harvard Theological Review*, 78 (1985), pp. 301–25.

108. See, for example, Mk. 10.35–37; Lk. 12.53, 14.26.

109. See Meggitt, *Paul, Poverty and Survival*, pp. 168–9.

110. Cf. Mk. 10.42; Mt. 20.25.

111. Meggitt, *Paul, Poverty and Survival*, pp. 169–75.

112. J. Nelson Kraybill, *Imperial Cult and Commerce in John's Apocalypse* (Sheffield: Sheffield Academic Press, 1996), pp. 72–80, 221.

113. See, for example, Pliny, *Epistles* 10.96; Origen, *Against Celsus* 3.55. For a useful study of this see Margaret MacDonald's work, *Early Christian Women and Pagan Opinion* (Cambridge: Cambridge University Press, 1996).

114. The relative liberalism of Asia Minor and Egypt is particularly notable. See M. T. Boatwright, 'Plancia Magna of Perge: Women's Roles and Status in Asia Minor', in S. Pomeroy (ed.), *Women's History and Ancient History* (Chapel Hill: University of North Carolina Press, 1991), pp. 249–72; D. Hobson, 'Women as Property Owners in Roman Egypt', *Transactions of the American Philological Association*, 113 (1983), pp. 311–21 and, 'The Role of Women in the Economic Life of Roman Egypt: A Case Study From First Century Tebtunis', *Echos du monde classique / Classical Views*, 28 (1984), pp. 373–90. In Asia Minor an unusual prominence had long been given to women, a point first made by O. Baunstein, *Die politische Wirksamkeit der griechischen Frau: eine Nachwirkung Orgriechischen Mutterrechts* (Leipzig: unpublished dissertation, 1911).

Printed in the United Kingdom
by Lightning Source UK Ltd.
2855